Westminste
the indispensable guide

Ian Collins

Cartoons by Tony Hall

JARROLD

Other titles in the Humour Series available from Jarrold Colour Publications:

Vicar's World by Patrick Forbes and Bill Ritson
Whine and Dine by Lesley and Cris de Boos
Racey Bits by Mark Siggers and Chris Williams

ISBN 0-7117-0351-5

First published in Great Britain, 1988

Designed and produced by
Parke Sutton Limited, 8 Thorpe Road,
Norwich NR1 1RY
for
Jarrold Colour Publications,
Barrack Street, Norwich NR3 1RT

Printed in England by
The Eastern Press Ltd., Reading

About the author

Ian Collins

Ian Collins has been a keen student of politics since a teenager, when he was one of four people who turned up for a public meeting addressed by his local MP, Clement Freud. Mercifully, he remembers, the audience was tripled during the Member's riveting speech. A family of eight called Gotobed arrived late.

After graduating with an honours degree in politics and economics from Manchester University in 1978, he trained as a journalist with the *Eastern Daily Press*. He now works in that newspaper's London office, and is a member of the Parliamentary Press Gallery.

Special thanks are due to the friends, relatives, colleagues and (not least) politicians who have so generously helped in the compilation of this book. They have made it fun to write and, I hope, fun to read.

Introduction

This book is written in affection, but with one eyebrow always raised at absurd and antique aspects of British politics. The strange stamp of the past is, of course, part of the charm of the Palace of Westminster – that amazing maze at the heart of this volume and our democracy. But major surgery may be pending.

It is too early to assess the likely impact of TV cameras in the Commons Chamber. The House of Lords has survived such scrutiny unscathed – thought not, it is to be hoped, because terminal tedium has struck the few who have been watching.

Those MPs who fought long and hard, and have finally failed to prevent filming of their debates, persist in fearing the imminent end of civilisation as they know it. But unseen on our screens, some MPs have long hammed it up. Neither can it be argued that the televised Commons will become cheaply commercialised, when Westminster already runs a hugely-profitable gift shop selling vast amounts of portcullis-stamped mints, wine and whisky, cufflinks and sundry other knick-knacks. The rot has already set in.

But the anti-TV lobby may have another point. How will viewers understand that when a whip tells the Speaker that the second reading of a Bill will take place 'tomorrow' he means 'in about a fortnight'; or that an Early Day Motion is unlikely to see the light of any day in the Commons Chamber; or that someone moving a reading for 'this day six months' means 'let's reject this rubbish now'? The choice is between subtitles, intrusive commentary or more procedural changes than three generations of Parliamentary reformers have managed.

So this book is intended as a light-hearted brief on the sometimes dotty ways of Parliament and politics, before they become boringly updated. It is also a review of some quaint quirks of our leading politicians past and present.

We should give thanks, I sincerely believe, for living in a land where we can laugh with and at our rulers. We are free to puncture the pomposity which is the first step to dictatorship.

However, if you never hear from me again, please send cards and chocolates care of the Tower of London.

Abroad

British politicians have tended to agree with George V that 'Abroad is bloody'. At best a patronising sympathy is extended to anyone with the misfortune to have been born a foreigner.

Ireland, France and Australia have drawn the most withering scorn. And Margot Asquith, whose husband led the last Liberal Government, spoke for many when she said: 'What a pity when Christopher Columbus discovered America that he ever mentioned it.'

It seems only fair, therefore, that foreigners should return our sentiment. When asked what he thought of Western civilisation, Mahatma Gandhi answered: 'I think it would be a very good idea'.

But Britons are at times prepared to suspend their prejudice. For example, the hit of our Queen's Coronation was the ample Queen of Tonga. Defying teeming rain, the massive monarch drove to Westminster Abbey in an open carriage so that she could wave to the crowds lining the route. Beside her sat a mystery man, less than half her size.

'Who is that little chap with her?' asked a friend of Noel Coward, as they watched the Coronation procession on TV.

The playwright famed for the sardonic quip replied: 'That's her lunch.'

Abseiling Lesbians

A dramatically down-to-earth display in the House of Lords occurred when a gay group threw ropes from the public gallery and abseiled into the Chamber below in a curious protest against a proposed ban on local authority promotion of homosexuality.

Rousing from their slumbers, one or two disoriented peers thought they were being treated to a leftover spectacle from the Royal Tournament.

Agent The person who usually gets no credit for an electoral victory, but who is always blamed for a defeat. An agent must ensure that campaign spending stays within the law, drill droves of untrained volunteers and calm or cheer the candidate, depending on whether the hopeful politician is in the manic or depressive phase of the illness.

Between elections, if a paid party employee, the agent must keep the electoral machine well-oiled, coax reluctant members to stand in 'hopeless' council seats (which, to their alarm, they often win) and operate as the eyes and ears of the MP. He or she is also likely to suffer severe stomach problems due to a compulsory diet of coffee mornings and cheese and wine evenings, and to suffer nightmares in which they have forgotten to open the constituency fete.

Aitken, Jonathan Powerful business baron and troublesome Tory MP from the Beaverbrook clan, Jonathan Aitken (Thanet South) was briefly best-known as a suitor of Carol Thatcher. Until her mum disapproved. For the blue-blooded blade dared to quip that the newish Prime Minister knew little about foreign affairs. 'She probably thinks that Sinai is the plural of sinus,' he joked, waving a Cabinet career goodbye.

Venturing beyond the jungle of TV-AM, Mr Aitken is now exploring less hazardous commercial concerns. That way he should at least reduce the danger of having glasses of wine thrown over him by grudge-bearing technicians taking their cue from Anna Ford.

Alcohol A favourite fuel of some of our more spirited politicians, though the demon drink has caused the downfall of a few of them. Occasionally literally. One stumbler was Lord George-Brown. Labour's former deputy leader said in his own defence: 'Most British statesmen have either drunk too much or womanised too much. I never fell into the second category.'

The Palace of Westminster is a law unto itself as far as permitted drinking hours are concerned. It is possible to get a drink at some bar or other as long as the House is sitting – all night if needs be. Though few MPs appear obviously the worse for wear after visiting the House refreshment outlets, extra noise and excitement during the last hour of an acrimonious debate – dubbed 'post-prandial euphoria' by Nye Bevan – may indeed indicate that certain people have supped and suppered well.

One Tory Member used to ask three questions at Question Time, down three large gins in the Smoking Room and then head for home unless there was a three-line whip. And a

Labour MP used to boast that his day had been wasted if he had not managed to imbibe 18 pints of beer in the Strangers' Bar.

Some think the danger and damage of alcohol is anyway much exaggerated. Two decades ago, Democrat Edmund Muskie withdrew as a United States vice-presidential candidate at a tearful Press conference, after reports that his wife had a drink problem. Harold Macmillan (later Lord Stockton) told his friends that Mr Muskie should have stuck it out. 'Come, come,' said one. 'What would you have done if your wife had been accused of being a drunk?'

Supermac replied 'I would have said "You should have seen her mother".'

Alliance A much discredited word, now replaced by Gang Warfare.

All-Night Sittings Westminster's weird working hours sometimes see MPs toiling all through the night in marathon debate. Such a procedure can cause a loss of sleep, tempers and the following day's business. It also creates havoc at home.

One MP, detained at a series of all-night sittings, found his wife doubting his excuse. Arriving at his house one early morning he found a note which read: 'The day before yesterday you came home yesterday morning, yesterday you came home this morning, so if today you come home tomorrow morning you will find that I left you yesterday.'

Ambition 'Whenever a man has cast a longing eye on offices, a rottenness begins in his conduct.' (Thomas Jefferson)

Answers If there is skill in framing a Parliamentary question, there is genius in an adequate answer – one which does not lie or deliberately mislead, or reveal what the Minister or spokesman wants to remain concealed.

A.J. Balfour put it this way: 'It has always been desirable to tell the truth, but seldom if ever necessary to tell the whole truth.'

There is a story of a Minister who was travelling with his private secretary to an engagement in the country, but whose driver lost the way. Stopping a passer-by, the chauffeur asked: 'Where are we?'

'In a car,' came the curt reply.

The civil servant mused: 'That, Minister, is the perfect Parliamentary answer. It is accurate, it is brief and it tells the questioner nothing he didn't know already.'

Apoplexy There is a lot of this about in politics, though sufferers aim to ensure that it breaks out only behind closed doors.

Ashdown, Paddy As a Royal Marine Commando, the young Paddy Ashdown (SLD Leader, Yeovil) learned useful devices for his later political career – such as how to surprise and garotte the enemy at dead of night.

Soon after his election to the Commons, the highflier with the film star looks greeted Ulster MP John Hume (SDLP, Foyle) like a long-lost friend. Mr Hume, a veteran civil rights activist, couldn't quite place the face. He was then astonished to be told: 'Don't you remember me? I once arrested you!'

Indian-born of Irish parents (half Roman Catholic, half Protestant) and Hong-Kong-schooled, cosmopolitan Mr Ashdown is a disarmer with an army background. He plays his cards close to his chest. In short, he is an enigma as inscrutable as the Chinese, with whom he can converse in fluent Mandarin.

Avebury, Lord Liberal Lord Avebury who, as Eric Lubbock, won a famous Orpington by-election only to lose the seat a few years later, is delighted when told that he looks a real dog's dinner. It isn't simply that the bicycling Buddhist peer is no study in sartorial elegance. His dearest wish has been that his body should one day be fed to the inmates of Battersea Dogs' Home – after first being advertised by his colleague Sir Clement Freud, perhaps. But sadly the fussy canines, or rather their squeamish keepers, have turned him down.

Bouncing back from this cruel blow, Lord Avebury now hopes that his corpse will help sustain the fishes of the sea or the worms of the meadow, and he doesn't much mind which.

Baker, Kenneth

The constant smile on the face of Kenneth Baker (Conservative, Mole Valley) suggests that this Cheshire cat of British politics has noticed the opinion polls putting him a favourite to follow Mrs Thatcher into Downing Street.

Having single-handedly revived the once-flagging sales of Brylcream, the sleek – some would say oily – politician is now struggling manfully to control the nation's illiteracy rates.

But will his education reforms work? Will young Britons grow to understand, and even to love, the marvels of modern maths? The Minister is confident that they will.

Unfortunately, being a Baker, he is also likely to believe that two half-dozens make thirteen.

Banks, Tony One of Labour's brightest and brashest MPs, left-winger Tony Banks (Newham North West) was offered *The Spectator's* Backbencher of the Year award for a string of witty speeches and interventions. But the man who once fumed about a Tory bias on *The Archers* felt unable to accept a tribute from such a conservative journal (so it was shared by anti-secrecy Tories Jonathan Aitken and Richard Shepherd).

Here is a sample of the Banks banter, as recorded in *Hansard:*

> **Mr Tony Banks:** Is not the Chancellor of the Exchequer (Nigel Lawson) insulting the House by refusing to come here and make a statement on what is clearly a matter of grave significance for the economy? Not only does the Rt. Hon. Gentleman physically resemble Nero, but he is clearly adopting the same attitude. Will you confirm, Mr Speaker, that you have the power to order the fat bounder to be dragged here from the dinner table?
>
> **Mr Speaker:** Order. First, I have not that power. Secondly, I dislike that expression, which I ask the Honourable Gentleman to withdraw.
>
> **Mr Banks:** In that case, Mr Speaker, I shall say 'the corpulent bounder'.
>
> **Mr Speaker:** That is almost as bad.

The former Greater London Council firebrand has also been at the receiving end of some acid humour. As on the following occasion (*Hansard* again):

> **Mr Tony Banks:** I wish to push the Secretary of State a little further. When can we expect an announcement? I have twice brought my sponge bag and twice I have returned home early. My wife clearly thinks that I am having an unsuccessful affair.
>
> **Mr Nicholas Ridley:** I really do not think that I can be held responsible for the disappointment to Mrs Banks.

Bar of the House Members are not allowed to speak outside the Bar, which consists of two rods which can be drawn across the ends of the benches to form the boundary of the House of Commons

Chamber opposite the Speaker's chair. Once inside, like habitués of other bars, they tend to become rather talkative.

The House has the authority to call to the Bar people indicted for breach of privilege. They are accompanied by the Serjeant at Arms with the Mace, a combination far more intimidating than any policeman and his truncheon. Such sinners used to have to kneel but are now allowed to stand. The rule was relaxed after one miscreant, on rising from his knees after being censured, brushed the dust from his clothes and declared: 'What a damned dirty House!'

Thus it was decided that to continue the practice would have meant risking further contempts of Parliament, as well as giving grave offence to the cleaners.

But some visitors assume that the phrase covers the watering-holes of Westminster, of which there is a thirst-quenching quantity. . . .

Bars of the House

The House of Lords has three dining rooms, in one of which guests may be entertained; three bar lounges; and the splendid Cholmondeley Room (named after a Lord Great Chamberlain), which leads on to the Terrace and is a favourite venue for cocktail parties and receptions.

One of the bars, known simply as 'the Lords' Bar' is the most democratic hostelry in the Palace: anyone employed in the building, as well as Members of both Houses, can adjourn there.

The Commons Refreshment Department, which serves up to 3,500 meals a day when the House is sitting, offers subsidised food and a celebrated wine list. It is responsible for eighteen separate points of sale, in half of which visitors may be entertained. Guests can get into the Strangers' Dining Room, cafeteria and bar and the four Terrace dining rooms, where lunches, dinners and receptions sponsored by MPs on behalf of outside bodies have helped to put the department into profit.

Most restful of Westminster's dining rooms is the Harcourt Room. There, to help soothe away the strains and stresses of public life, and possibly to distract attention from the stodgy food, a harp is played.

Like the other non-Members, journalists are barred from the Members' dining room. On the other hand, MPs are admitted to the Press Gallery dining room, cafeteria and bar only as guests of accredited members of the Press Gallery.

Common ground for hacks and Housemen are Annie's Bar (named after a long-gone but legendary barmaid), the Terrace and the Strangers' Bar (also dubbed the Kremlin, due to its popularity with left-wing Labour MPs).

It is after visiting these latter places that an MP may discover, opening his newspaper the next day, that an evening drink with a journalist loosened his tongue just a little too much.

Baths The baths and showers in the House of Commons are where leftish Labour MPs rub shoulders with aristocratic Tories. The former like to give the public impression that they still do not have inside plumbing at home. The latter revel in a tribal ritual that reminds them of their public schools.

Beaumont-Dark, Anthony The Tory MP for Birmingham Selly Oak is devoted to gaming machines, curious causes and backbench revolts. Normally bully-boy whips treat him warily.

Past bees in the Beaumont-Dark bonnet have included a belief that Catholics should subsidise council housing because they oppose contraception and so tend to take up more space. He is now widely admired as a House of Commons character, who still generates excitement. At any moment he may go off again with a bang.

Beggar Me Some of the best political humour has been enacted without a word spoken. Take the scene recounted by Lord Mancroft in his witty memoirs. . .

The Conservative peer was serving at the War Office in 1942 when he was asked to go to Downing Street during the Prime Minister's absence, to bring war maps up to date. So one Saturday afternoon he was lying on the ante-room floor surrounded by the tools for the task, with his belt and hat discarded beside him – looking, perhaps, the very picture of a pavement artist.

Suddenly Winston Churchill, who had been thought to be at Chequers, careered through the room deep in conversation with an American general. The young Lord Mancroft hurriedly clambered to his feet, but was waved down again by the apparently preoccupied Premier as he headed into the Cabinet Office.

But at the door the great man paused. Looking back, he put his hand into his pocket, withdrew a penny and without a word tossed it into the Mancroft hat. Then he ambled away, with perhaps the merest flicker of a smile.

Beith, Alan If 'liberal' meant 'permissive', Alan Beith (SLD, Berwick-upon-Tweed) would never have joined the party. He is anti-drink, anti-porn and anti-tobacco. Just the man to win a sensational by-election after the call-girl-prompted resignation of Tory MP Lord Lambton in 1973.

Educationalist Mr Beith is a senior-teacher sort of chap, who wanted to become headmaster of his party. He is a tireless campaigner, a linguist who is able to explain the finer points of Liberalism to any Welsh or Danish speakers in his sprawling corner of Northumberland.

Decent, but not exactly dazzling, he approaches politics like a Methodist lay preacher. Which is exactly what he is.

Below the Gangway The gangway cuts across the Commons Chamber about half-way down, and can be seen as a cut-off point for effective political power.

Positions below it are generally occupied by minority groups and party dissidents. Thus, on the Opposition side, David Owen must sit with Beast of Bolsover Dennis Skinner bawling in his ear.

Best, Keith A warning to Westminster. Keith Best surprised himself and everyone else with the biggest swing of the 1979 General Election, to pull off the first-ever Tory triumph in Anglesey (Ynys Mon). The victor missed the historic count as he was anxiously defending a seat on Brighton council at the time.

But the mould-breaking barrister fell foul of the law when he used variations of his name and addresses to overclaim for British Telecom shares. He left Westminster before the last election, and briefly landed in jail.

Keith Best has bequeathed a lasting legacy. All politicians now check their claims and returns with extra care.

Big Ben Big Ben gives the lie to the popular sneer that you can never rely on anything at Westminster. With a pile of old pennies perfectly weighting its balancing mechanism, the towering Victorian timepiece is as regular as clockwork. Its 13½-ton bell strikes the quarter-hours with reassuring (if deafening) precision.

The tower itself contains a room, under the clock, designed to hold villains offending against the order, dignity and privilege of the House of Commons. The last man locked up there, in 1880, was freethinker Charles Bradlaugh who, on his election as MP for Northampton, refused to take the oath of allegiance to the Queen.

Bradlaugh claimed, as a non-believer, his right to affirm loyalty rather than swearing it on the Bible. Luckily, this was finally conceded. Otherwise the tower cell, or more likely the Police

Room next to Westminster Hall, would be bursting with Labour MPs who now claim a similar right.

Big Benn Tony Benn, rather than his Ealing councillor son Hilary.

Mr Benn Snr may have reduced his parent-given name of Anthony Wedgwood Benn, and renounced his hereditary peerage, but he retains another family tradition by staying teetotal.

Or perhaps that should be tea-total. For the veteran left-wing MP (Labour, Chesterfield) can down dozens of cups of beverage in a single day, and has been given a special time-saving pint mug in the Commons Tea Room.

Billericay The good voters of Billericay, Essex, must be used to odd antics from their MP. Before the last election they were represented by spanker Harvey Proctor.

Now they have Superwoman Teresa Gorman, who sounds off on all manner of surprising subjects. She swears by the benefits of hormone replacement, for instance (while reducing her official age by as much as ten years).

Other MPs keep dogs, parrots or even monkeys – and Ken Livingstone is very fond of his fleet of newts. But Mrs Gorman waxes lyrical about the delights of the humble *humbicus terrestris*. 'I love my little earthworms,' she coos. 'I stroke their tummies and it makes them relax.'

The MP has been quick to defend her pets against what she perceives as dire danger. She gushes: 'They busy themselves about the place in a thoroughly desirable Thatcherite way. The trouble is that they are now under threat from the Common Market and the farmers with their dreadful nitrates.'

This is no laughing matter, Mrs Gorman insists. She adds the warning: 'Once the worm turns, we've all had it.'

Bills

Bills dominate political life. Not the sort that appear in brown envelopes, although this variety has driven the odd MP to bankruptcy and out of the House of Commons. Parliamentary Bills are the stuff from which laws are made.

Every legislative proposal begins as a private or public Bill. Private Bills affect individuals, corporations or local interests. Most, however, are public and are introduced by a Minister. Alternatively, a few days each year are set aside for ballot-topping backbenchers to propose Private Members' Bills. Like pools winners, however, the lucky few often find that their sudden riches are tricked out of them by smooth talkers, and they never make the statute book.

When the Clerk announces a Bill's short title, the proposer takes a bow and the measure is regarded as 'read a first time'. The Speaker then asks, 'What date second reading?' And a whip replies 'Tomorrow' – code for 'about a fortnight'.

Second reading sees a broad debate on principles. If hostile to the proposals, the opposition will vote against them or move a reading 'this day six months' (meaning much the same thing).

A government Bill is rarely voted down. Loss of a key measure would be taken as a vote of no confidence and the Prime Minister might be forced to seek a dissolution of Parliament and a general election. Whips work flat out to avoid such an inconvenience.

Once through its second reading, a Bill goes to a standing committee of 16–50 MPs for detailed study. On rare and crucial issues all 650 Members form the committee. This procedure invites delay, which is why governments loathe it and oppositions love it.

Out of committee, a Bill as amended is reported to the House and may be further changed before its third and final reading on broad principles. Afterwards it is endorsed with the obscure phrase 'Soit baillé aux Seigneurs' (Norman-French for 'Let it be delivered to the Lords'). The Clerk then carries the master copy to the Upper House, where it is subjected to much the same process it has just survived in the Commons.

A Bill amended by the Lords returns to MPs for further consideration. Most tidying changes will be accepted, but Ministers often try to get others dropped. If peers persist in contested amendments, an identical Bill can be passed in the Commons in the next session – provided one year has elapsed – without lordly consent. Peers have to hope that high-handed governments will get their come-uppance from the voters. 'Money' Bills, dealing with public finance, are the exception. The Lords cannot delay them beyond a month. MPs like to pull the nation's purse strings.

All Bills became Acts – the law of the land, entered in the statute book – on receiving Royal Assent, when the Queen signs on the proverbial dotted line.

Black Rod The Gentleman Usher of the Black Rod – fetchingly clad in tunic, knee-breeches, silk stockings, silver-buckled shoes and cocked hat – is a senior House of Lords official whose origins date from Edward III's day. The decree establishing the post said it must go to 'a gentleman famous in arms and blood'. No, not a party politician but a retired military man.

The first holder of the office, William Whitehorse, received 12d (5p) a day for life, for walking in front of the King carrying an ebony staff. If anyone abused the Order of the Garter, he was tapped on the shoulder with the rod and expelled, whereupon the Gentleman Usher received £5. Not a bad bonus at the time. And even today, in his only surviving court function, Black Rod still walks in front of the Queen during Garter ceremonies at Windsor. But he hasn't had to tap a subversive shoulder for ages.

Similar in role to the Serjeant at Arms of the House of Commons, he or his deputy (the Yeoman Usher) controls admission of visitors when the House is sitting. He also commits those guilty of breach of privilege or contempt.

Black Rod, in accordance with ancient custom, is sent to desire the attendance of MPs in the House of Lords at the Opening and Proroguing (closure) of Parliament. And he has the door slammed in his face for his trouble (*see* **Swearing In**).

Blue Book Popular name for a Government publication bound, because of its bulk, in a blue cover. Or an example of a certain sort of literature which frequently finds its way into secret corners of Westminster, and even into the loos. Just such a publication (shredded) once brought about a blockage of the entire Parliamentary sewage system.

When quoting from this type of text in the Commons Chamber, an MP is well advised first to make sure that the volume falls into the former category, rather than the latter.

Blue Rinse A popular form of final preparation by female delegates to Tory conferences, who may also be more intent on polishing their dance steps than their speeches.

Bottomley, Peter Roads and traffic Minister Peter Bottomley (Conservative, Eltham), gained valuable experience while working as a lorry driver in the 1960s.

The MP is also uniquely qualified to make himself heard in the House of Commons – he was briefly a barker at Battersea funfair.

Boundary Commission Just when you have secured a tame selection committee and a safe seat, and are looking forward to a leisurely Parliamentary career, a decision of the Boundary Commissioners can put you out on your ear. Many are the mighty who have fallen in this way.

The Boundary Commission (or rather one each for England, Scotland, Wales and Northern Ireland) is a permanent body reporting to the Home Secretary every ten to fifteen years on the redistribution of seats. Population shifts mean that the political map must be redrawn and constituencies altered, invented or abolished.

In recent years the movement away from the inner cities and towards the suburbs and shires has given the Conservatives anything but the blues, while making Labour see red.

So the ambitious young politician seeking a secure future must ideally find a safe seat within a cluster of strongholds – and become well known and liked in the lot. With the Boundary Commissioners ever in action, the youthful hopeful never knows when such support will be needed.

Breaking the Code What is said in politics can differ from what is meant, even to the point of being the exact opposite. Here are some choice examples . . . complete with truthful translations:

'A brilliant mind. . .'
The speaker agrees with me. If 'dogmatic', he disagrees.

'Should go far. . .'
The kiss of death to new and promising MPs.

'There is no alternative'
Tina was a popular figure of Tory speech in the early 1980s, and she may be recalled from retirement once more when the going gets tough.

'A frank exchange'
Blows were traded.

'I hear what you say'
But nothing will be done about it.

'Safe in our hands'
Butter-fingers!

'To be honest'
Three little words politicians insert into certain sentences to underline their candour, but which merely serve to stress the dubiousness of their other utterances.

'May I say. . .'
Try stopping me.

'Poorly presented. . .'
Are you mad? This disastrous policy must be dropped at once.

'In my judgement. . .'
A harebrained scheme is about to be announced.

'I'm lost for words'
You will wait a long time to hear this in politics.

'Posterity'
Somewhere after the next election.

'With the greatest respect. . .'
Stand by to be grossly insulted.

'Badly advised. . .'
The Minister is an idiot.

Brittan, Leon

Maggie-loyalist Leon Brittan resigned as Trade and Industry Secretary during the Westland saga of 1986. He expected to be recalled to the Cabinet after a brief interval but – following a long silence – has now been appointed an EEC Commissioner. Can-carriers are sometimes rewarded.

Brown, Gordon

Labour Treasury spokesman Gordon Brown (Dunfermline East) is one of a select band of MPs with a clear grasp of economics. If he ever becomes Chancellor, he will not need to follow the example of one predecessor, Jim Callaghan, who travelled twice weekly to Oxford for lessons in the subject.

A former friend of Princess Marguerite of Rumania, the power-hungry Labour MP hopes that he too is not part of a displaced dynasty.

Brown, Ron Action man Ron Brown (Labour, Edinburgh Leith, Tripoli North and Kabul Central) has a reckless record. He damaged the House of Commons Mace after dropping it to the floor (for which he was suspended and ordered to pay repair costs of £1,500), and in Scotland once lunged at Mrs Thatcher waving a pay slip (for which he was fined £50).

This leftist class warrior says 'I have never gone in for popularity'. It is true that the Labour leadership loathes him. Mr Brown has gone down a storm, however, in Moscow, Libya and Afghanistan.

Browne, John John Browne (Conservative, Winchester) once warned of the danger of overcrowding and boredom in his local prison. His ex-wife later faced a possible jail term for failing to meet a huge divorce settlement (after the MP's admitted adultery). Luckily she was given further time to pay.

Bruinvels, Peter A rent-a-quote seat-hunting ex-MP, who has whiled away some idle hours penning religious copy for that devout journal, *The Sun*.

Hanger-flogger Tory Peter Bruinvels would also like to be a public executioner (though as a marksman, he prefers firing squads).

Budgen, Nicholas Grandson of the Shropshire parson who baptised Enoch Powell, Nick Budgen (Conservative, Wolverhampton South West) has inherited the Tory-turned-Ulster Unionist's former Black Country seat – as well as most of his opinions.

Budget The name of Sir Geoffrey Howe's dog. Or the day, shortly before the start of each financial year, dreaded by tipplers and tobacco fiends. Some light up or drink up at twice their normal pace to cope with the shock.

Budget comes from the word 'budge'. This, of course, is something that Chancellors – and all other politicians – dislike doing.

More to the point however, 'budge' is also the Anglicised form of the French 'bouge', meaning 'small bag'; and it could derive from a 1733 cartoon which showed Prime Minister Robert Walpole explaining his financial measures like a quack doctor, opening a bag filled with medicines and charms.

Nowadays the Chancellor of the Exchequer produces his magic potions from a battered red despatch box, but the principle remains the same.

In the Budget, the Chancellor – Britain's Finance Minister – gives a usually rosy report of the previous year's accounts,

B Budget

followed by curious reasoning as to why there should nevertheless be swingeing tax changes in one area or another.

Preparation is shrouded in great secrecy. But with armies of leak-detectors and computer-code-breakers these days, key proposals stay hidden for about ten minutes after being first mooted.

The sport of Budget speculation centres on alcohol in more than simply the taxing sense. 'With what will the Minister lubricate his vocal cords?' Westminster-watchers wonder. For the Chancellor is the only MP allowed to break a ban on boozing in the Commons Chamber, and then only during his Budget speech. It helps to add sparkle to dull delivery.

Nigel Lawson is a devotee of spritzer (English white wine with carbonated Malvern water), whereas his predecessor, Sir

Geoffrey Howe, tippled on gin and tonic. Another former Tory Chancellor, Derick Heathcoat-Amory, mixed milk, honey and rum.

Although Denis Healey favoured diluted brandy, other Labour Chancellors have stayed off the strong stuff altogether. Jim Callaghan chose quinine (tonic) water and Sir Stafford Cripps plain old tap-water.

In the last century, Gladstone was sustained during his marathon 1853 four-and-threequarter-hour Budget speech by a disgusting concoction of sherry and beaten egg. In contrast, his great rival Disraeli raced through his 1867 Budget revelations in a record 45 minutes. Aided by brandy and water.

Burke's Peerage The somewhat unfortunate title refers to the original author, not the contents, of this regularly-updated guide. Since John Burke first thought up the idea, in 1826, it has offered a complete genealogical and heraldic history of the nation's blue blood – flowing through Royals, peers, baronets and knights.

The text has proved essential reading for matrons determined that their debutante daughters should marry a Barbara Cartland hero, or at least acquire a stately home.

Butcher, John John Butcher (Coventry South West), a failed rock musician turned Tory Minister, had to apologise for accusing northerners of being 'workshy'. His angry colleagues above the Trent saw their majorities fading fast after such a slur.

Since the arrival of Edwina Currie, Mr Butcher's pro-southern prejudices have been rather overshadowed.

Canvassing The political equivalent of double-glazing salesmen, gypsy fortune-tellers and ice cream vendors. Selling policies and candidates can be the hardest retailing operation of all.

Indeed, so great are the potential pitfalls that canvassers risk losing more support than they gain. But all parties do it, and none dares to be first to drop out.

A major hazard of canvassing is four-legged, sabre-toothed and usually growling. For behind many garden walls lurk horrible hounds of the Baskervilles. . . or their more condensed cousins. One poor candidate was attacked by a ferocious terrier, which bit into his coat and doggedly refused to let go. The lady of the house came to the door, yelling at her pet to stop. Until, spotting the colour of the candidate's rosette, she changed her mind. 'Eat him!' she ordered.

Cut-glass voices drifting across council tenements can meet

with a disappointing response, as can heavy urban accents in the shires. But fools and fervent canvassers rush in. . .

During the 1906 election campaign, when the Tories were heading for their heaviest defeat, the lovely young wife of an aristocratic MP was canvassing a rare mining village in her husband's rural constituency. 'I am canvassing for your husband's vote on behalf of my husband,' she said in clipped tones to the woman who answered one lowly door.

'Hey, Bert, it's Her Ladyship wanting your vote for her husband,' shouted the woman.

'Tell her I'll nay vote for a man who never gets up before dinner time,' came the angry reply from the back room.

At this, the beautiful young canvasser pushed her way into the house to defend her husband from the charge of sloth. As she entered the back room, the miner was rising stark naked from his tin bath.

Seeing her speechless distress, he said kindly: 'Nay lass, now I've seen you, you can tell your husband if I were him I'd stay in bed all day!'

Carlton Club

Grandest of London's political clubs, the Carlton in St James's Street is just a stone's throw from the Reform Club. The distance may have been tested with actual rocks, as members of the two bodies were once bitter foes.

Even today the Carlton Club retains its reputation as a haven for right-wing Tory grandees, and many important Conservative gatherings have been held there. Countless plots have been hatched within the hallowed walls.

The club hosted a special reception to mark Mrs Thatcher's feat in becoming the longest-serving Premier this century. The bash doubled up as a retirement do for Lord Whitelaw, who was forced to quit as deputy premier on doctor's orders.

Mingling over drinks, Mrs Thatcher took pains to scotch rumours that she alone had never really appreciated the peer's steadying hand. 'Every Prime Minister needs a Willie,' the Prime Minister was heard to declare.

Casting Vote

If a Commons vote is tied, the Speaker can cast the decider. But the impartiality of his office obliges him, where possible, to vote in such a way that the House can look at the issue again.

He must also give his reasons for choosing one side over the other. One 17th century Speaker who backed a crucial and otherwise tied vote to adjourn a session, earned his place in history for admitting that he had done so because he was 'very hungry'.

Catching the Speaker's Eye

Rather than some grisly game of anatomical cricket, 'catching the speaker's eye' explains the curious sight of MPs bursting upwards from their benches in energetic bids to speak.

The first Member-in-Motion spotted from the Chair is supposed to be the one called to spout forth – but in practice the Speaker uses discretion, noting the will of the House and the desire for balanced debate.

Otherwise the unmissable Cyril Smith (SLD, Rochdale) would have a big advantage over punier and greyer men.

Chalker, Linda

The first divorcée to be selected as a Tory candidate, Linda Chalker (Wallasey) has declined to take her second husband's name. Had she done so, we would now be referring to the bright blonde bicyclist as Linda Landa. Roedean's ex-head girl has been a godsend at the Foreign Office as one of our few politicians who can speak foreign languages, as well as being more than averagely fluent in English.

Chamber

If an air of confrontation hangs over the Commons Chamber, it is not helped by the rectangular shape and the rows of benches starkly facing each other. In contrast, continental assemblies – where coalitions abound – sit in semi-circles; but they may also encourage a speeded-up game of musical chairs, which has given Italy a new government on average almost annually since the war.

Britain plays musical chairs in its politics in another sense: there simply aren't enough Commons seats to go round – 480 to be exact and 650 bottoms. This is not due to government spending cutbacks, but has been a deliberate design.

Churchill, speaking in a 1943 debate on rebuilding the bomb-blitzed Chamber, said it

> “should not be big enough to contain all its Members at once without overcrowding, and there should be no question of every Member having a separate seat reserved for him. If the House is big enough to contain all its Members, nine-tenths of its debates will be conducted in the depressing atmosphere of an almost empty or half empty Chamber.”

The result of such advice has been for half the debates to be conducted in a depressingly-empty chamber, and others when it is fractiously full to bursting. On key occasions – such as a Budget speech, the State Opening of Parliament or during scandals – MPs anxious for a good seat must camp out like tennis fans for the Men's Final at Wimbledon or the most eager bargain-hunters in the January sales.

Churchill added: 'The essence of good House of Commons speaking is the conversational style. . . But the conversational style requires a fairly small space, and there should be on great occasions a sense of crowd and urgency.'

The point at which a 'sense of crowd and urgency' turns into a mob riot is eagerly awaited by TV viewers, who have come to expect high drama when the peak-time cameras roll.

Channon, Paul Born with a golden spoon in his mouth, seasoned Minister Paul Channon (Conservative, Southend West) inherited a fortune and a safe Tory seat previously held in turn by his father, grandmother and grandfather.

On the Guinness heir's adoption as a Conservative candidate, when an Oxford student aged 23, his grandmother congratulated the selection panel. 'I think you have done right by backing a colt when you know the stable it was trained in,' she said. Plainly nepotism finds favour in this family.

Chequers One of Buckinghamshire's most stately piles has been used as the country residence of the Prime Minister since Lloyd George's day. It is intended as an away-from-it-all rural retreat, where the Premier can entertain favourites and visiting foreign leaders in relaxed seclusion.

The calm and charm of Chequers was shattered for a time in the 1950s, when the view frequently included a neighbour's washing line loaded with knickers. Lady Eden, the then Premier's wife, was mortified. But Lady Violet Bonham-Carter, Asquith's daughter, dismissed this briefs encounter with the words: 'If I were Lady Eden, instead of objecting to it, I would ask for it to come nearer. I think it would help me to entertain my distinguished, but often rather heavy, visitors.'

Children It is often said that the offspring of politicians have a bad deal. Fractured family life is one casualty of a career spent chasing public office.

Revolts against parental values are common, with the colour of the family politics frequently dyed a different hue by the young rebels. Foreign Secretary Geoffrey Howe, for instance, must have winced when his son became a press officer for CND.

Nigella Lawson, named after her Chancellor dad, was rather rude about Mrs Thatcher when reviewing Shere Hite's *Women and Love* for *The Sunday Times*. She wrote: 'We are not by some biological imperative the more caring sex. Crude proof of this is easily supplied by the behaviour of Britain's most famous female.' Pater and Prime Minister cannot have been amused.

There may be some compensation for neglected offspring if their political parents are rich. Lord Rothschild once curtly dismissed a cabman who complained that the tip he had just been given was half that received from Rothschild's son some days earlier.

'I know,' said the peer. 'My son has a millionaire for a father. I haven't.'

Chiltern Hundreds

If you want to know the way to the Chiltern Hundreds of Stoke, Desborough and Burnham, or the Manor of Northstead, simply follow the exit signs. The destinations are sought by MPs seeking a way out of Westminster.

Rather than saying 'I quit' and heading home, a Member wishing to resign has to follow the quaint custom of applying to be steward or bailiff of one of these antique areas. Both are nominally offices of profit under the Crown, which MPs cannot hold and keep their seats. So they retire gracefully.

Should you think this practice silly, be advised that the House of Commons' custom has moved smartly into the 20th century. In Victorian times, resigning MPs could apply for stewardship of the Manors of East Hendred and Hempholme as well.

Clarke, Kenneth Moderate Tory MP Kenneth Clarke (Rushcliffe) has made the inner sanctum of the Cabinet on merit, though there is some doubt as to whether Mrs T regards him as 'one of us'. The Premier may recall that he used his maiden speech to thank her, when she was Education Secretary, for a new school in his constituency. But she will certainly not have forgotten the displeasure the young Heathite showed when she became Tory leader.

Class While party politics may be veering to right and left, the class make-up of the House of Commons is meeting in the middle.

Labour benches are no longer packed with horny-handed sons of toil, but with polytechnic lecturers anxious to disguise their bourgeois background. On the Tory side the Knights of the Shires have been ousted by suburbanites, who are as middle-class as their Labour opponents – but proud of it.

Of course, there are exceptions. Of 43 upper-crust Old Etonians in the Commons, two (Tam Dalyell and Mark Fisher) sit on the Labour side. And, led by Antonia Fraser's cousin Harriet Harman (Peckham), a sizeable number of Socialists from the lesser public schools brigade has traded the clipped tones of childhood for the South London accent which is now compulsory for advancement in the People's Party.

An earlier blue-blooded left-winger, Tom Driberg, had no qualms about his privileged past. As a Labour conference train began leaving Blackpool for London, several comrades waiting on the platform heard the unmistakable Driberg drawl from the buffet car. 'Do you seriously mean to tell me that British Rail doesn't serve oysters?' he was asking in amazement.

Clerk of the House Despite Michael Foot's maxim that 'all is fair in love, war and Parliamentary procedure', the Clerk of the House and his substantial staff ensure that – in the latter case at least – complex rules are obeyed. Their Bible of office was compiled by a Clerk of the last century named Erskine May. Updated, it remains in constant use.

The Clerk's staff fall into several categories. Some sit in the Chamber and advise the Speaker or other MPs on procedure. Others work from what might be called the office of broken dreams. For they decide whether a Member's question is technically, procedurally and linguistically correct. Many are the brilliant ideas for outwitting Ministers that have gone no further.

Another platoon of officials advises on acceptance of amendments to Bills, while still more cover the select committees of MPs that have mushroomed over the last decade. And though clerks of the overseas office are supposed to help the Mother of Parliament's offspring that have grown up since the end of empire, they often find that such advice is spurned as colonial interference. Nowadays they look more to Europe, where the antique and confrontational nature of the British Parliament needs a good deal of explaining.

Clerks of the journal office staff the lobby desks, marking off Members as they vote. Their boss also sits as Clerk of the Committee of Privileges, which meets when Members feel that someone has besmirched their integrity or sobriety. The stick they can wield is used sparingly, but *The Guardian*'s sketch-writer, Andrew Rawnsley, almost felt it when he wondered why so few Labour MPs had attended a certain debate.

'The latest theory is the oldest,' he wrote. 'At work, once again, is the Westminster Triangle: drink, laziness and incompetence.' Teetotal MPs who had been slaving in committees at the time rose up in fury!

And finally there is the Clerk Administrator, to whom MPs are especially attached. He sees that papers for the day's Commons business arrive on their breakfast tables – and, through control of the fees office, that their salaries and expenses are met.

Collecting the Voices

Not auditions for the House of Commons choir, but the point at which the Speaker reads the motion at the end of a Commons debate and adds: 'As many as are of that opinion say Aye.' Supporters of the motion comply, then the Speaker continues: 'As many as are of the contrary opinion say No.'

Once the voices are collected, MPs may or may not divide into the voting lobbies.

Clearly this practice benefits Members who have trained in voice projection, while those unfortunates who often suffer from laryngitis may find themselves on the losing side more than most.

C Committee of Public Accounts

Committee of Public Accounts A select committee of MPs set up to ensure that all public money is spent as Parliament intended.

This body has been much criticised for performing merely a post-mortem function. But perhaps social reformer Sidney Webb provided it with a perfect defence when he said: 'The fact that post-mortem examination does nothing to keep the patient alive is no proof that the existence of a system of post-mortem examinations does not prevent murders.'

Communists Formed in London's Cannon Street Station Hotel in 1920, the Communist Party of Great Britain could now fit comfortably into a decent-sized bingo hall. Not that the comrades would ever consider sitting together, for they are deeply split.

The old party is chiefly fissured into factions. The first subscribes to the trendy magazine *Marxism Today*. These Filofax-carrying comrades like their Socialism diluted, preferably with champagne. The second band, of austere old-style Stalinists, are grouped around the *Morning Star* newspaper. They are still slavishly devoted to the Soviet Union, whose bulk order keeps their loss-making journal afloat.

These days, though retaining a foothold in certain trade unions, Communists of any shade come nowhere near to winning Parliamentary seats – or even saving deposits – under their own colours. There is thus the delicious irony that the only Communist spokesman at Westminster is Wogan Phillips, the hereditary peer Lord Milford. The octogenarian farmer from Gloucestershire, with an Eton-educated heir, remains touchingly loyal to the ideals of his youth.

Computers Most MPs, public bodies and thriving constituency parties are now computerised – lured by the idea of endless information at their finger tips. Practice can make imperfect, however.

Take the £70,000 computer recently installed at a health centre in Edwina Currie's home constituency of South Derbyshire. Remembering her NHS number, the Junior Minister confidently punched it on the keyboard. After an ominous pause, the screen offered the message 'Patient not known'.

Equally unhelpful was the computer acquired by the Westminster office of the then Liberal leader David Steel. One aide tapped in the two little words 'Margaret Thatcher', only to send the machine into hysterics. Lights flashed, buzzers blared. 'Please replace, please replace,' begged a caption on the silver screen.

Condoms With campaigns for safe sex finding all-party support, most MPs think the condom is a thoroughly good thing.

However in this, as in other sensitive areas, Nicholas Winterton (Conservative, Macclesfield) is an exception. He has fumed against the piles of discarded condoms that appear to litter his path, and has framed a furious Parliamentary question on research into the problem of throwaway protectives. The MP was informed by a straight-faced Environment Minister, Colin Moynihan, that tests had been conducted on the product, but it was still feared that 'biodegradability might affect performance'. Quite.

Condoms have, of course, been popular for ages past. Even so, there were many raised eyebrows at the recent claims by writer Theo Aronson, in his biography of Edward VII, *The King In Love*. The philandering monarch was said to have ordered condoms by the boxload.

And to make the Royal protectives appear respectable, the cartons carried portraits 'of the most irreproachable Victorian notables they could think of: staring starkly at each other across every box of condoms were Queen Victoria and Mr Gladstone'.

Conferences Party faithful who want to blend their annual autumn get-together with a late holiday head for spa or seaside towns. (Certain trade unions have even reached the Channel Islands.) The rules of these engagements stress the differences between, and sometimes within, each grouping.

For Labour and diehard Liberals, conferences are where grassroots activists press for major policy changes (which, if passed, are usually ignored by the leadership). In both gatherings, endless points of order tend to reduce debates to dire disorder. But for the Socialists, fiercely-fought topics can end in runaway voting victories, as one Trade Union delegate holds a 1¼-million block ballot in the palm of his raised hand.

For the Owenite SDP, the most middle-aged and middle-class grouping of the lot, the proceedings are typified by earnest debates and eager deference to doctor's orders.

Most impressive in its smooth stage-management is the Conservative conference. Many delegates, viewing the occasion chiefly as a social rather than a political event, are prepared to cheer any face they recognise – even if, as may happen when Michael Heseltine follows Nigel Lawson, the message being imparted varies sharply. Only the Home Secretary is greeted with a deafening silence when he argues against the return of the stocks, cane, rope and ducking stool.

Otherwise, the esctatic rally could be subtitled *Rhapsody in Blue* or *The Adoration of the Maggie*. The Tory conference's main problem is in knowing when to end its standing ovation for the Leaderine's carefully-prepared oratory.

Confidence Politicians usually lack little by way of confidence. Although Winston Churchill once described Clement Attlee as a modest little man with much to be modest about, most politicians – even if they have a great deal to be modest about – are bursting with self-esteem.

MPs might be divided between talkers and listeners. There are, say, roughly 640 in the first category, and ten in the second. The division was neatly summed up by an exchange involving the old Duke of Devonshire, who sat in the House of Commons as Lord Hartington. He turned to a colleague and declared: 'Oh, how I hate having to make a speech'.

'Oh, do you? I don't mind a bit,' his friend replied. 'I just can't bear listening.'

Woodrow Wyatt, journalist and former Labour MP, takes an opposite view to Lord Birkenhead, who held the opinion that it was impossible to make a good speech unless the speaker felt nervous beforehand. Woodrow Wyatt says:

> My moderate (public speaking) successes have come when I have floated forward on an unaccountable surge of self-confidence and well-being combined, I regret to say, with a belief that most of my audience are mentally inferior to myself. I most frequently achieved that happy state in the House of Commons.

Conflict of Interests

A grey area. MPs may not accept fees for professional services connected with the proceedings of Parliament. Neither may they vote in any matter in which they have a direct financial interest. It is also customary for an MP who has a personal interest in the subject under discussion to declare it.

Worries over the growing number of consultancies accepted by MPs, and the increasing activities of lobbyists, have led to the creation of a Register of MPs' interests which is open to public inspection. Professional fees or financial sponsorships, subsidised overseas visits, payments from foreign sources, and interests in land or property of substantial value should all be declared. A large number of tycoons has been revealed, chiefly on the Tory side, but any impropriety has stayed hidden.

The former Conservative and Ulster Unionist MP Enoch Powell declared such a register to be a gross violation of privacy and refused to make a return. His defeat at South Down at the last General Election spared Parliament the agony of deciding whether or not to do anything about it.

Conviction

> Margaret, never do things just because other people do them. Make up your mind about what you are going to do and persuade people to go your way.

None could claim that the dutiful daughter of Alderman Alf Roberts has not taken his advice to heart. The ghost of a Grantham grocer (who shares more than a name with the corner-shop magnate of Coronation Street) stalks in Downing Street.

And, perhaps tellingly, the Prime Minister's first response to the Toxteth riots of 1981 was: 'Oh, those poor shopkeepers'.

The Count

'Indeed you won the election. But I won the count.' The comment of Anastasio Somoza, former dictator of Nicaragua, illustrates the importance of careful counting. In Britain it is conducted by an impartial staff, led by a Returning Officer, in each constituency.

In safe seats the whole event may have the air of a foregone conclusion – save, possibly, for trauma over a lost deposit or two. In marginal divisions the atmosphere will be electric.

As the ballots are sorted into batches of 100, first to check the overall tally from each polling station and then to find the share for each contender, candidates distinguished by differing shades of rosette try to gauge from the gush of paper slips whether they will have a job for the next five years. Their minders shadow each counter, all too aware that the wrong name on the top of a bundle could deliver 99 votes to the enemy.

The piles are then collected and stacked in thousands on a side table. The parties watch in horror as the pace of each growing column varies, and the lead may switch to and fro.

A sensible candidate, if wishing to avoid inflaming an ulcer or suffering a heart attack, arrives at the last possible moment. The agent should have been told to give an agreed signal on the likely outcome. But sometimes this sign is forgotten in the rush of events, and the latecomer is in shock when the result is announced.

A candidate may be ahead in votes on the table, only to lose on postal votes. And really close results can hinge on mauled or spoilt ballot papers. Amid a scrum of agents and candidates, a Returning Officer is likely to accept ticks instead of crosses as valid. But the political hopefuls may also find that the odd elector has sent them a message to Something Off. This will be their only moment of solidarity in a divisive evening.

At last, usually in the early hours of the morning, the candidates are called together to learn the will of the people. If the verdict is extremely close, the loser demands a recount. There may even be recounts of recounts. The smallest majority since universal suffrage was at Ilkeston, Derbyshire, in 1931 when, after much checking, a National Labour candidate beat his Labour opponent by two votes.

With the result announced, and cheers and jeers subsiding, the winner makes a speech congratulating staff on the conduct of the count, thanks helpers and tries to resist a snide swipe at vanquished opponents.

Losers may then choke back tears to say a few words. But the philosophical reflect that a sound second-place could ensure them a better prospect next time.

Critchley, Julian

Witty moderate Julian Critchley (Conservative, Aldershot) was unmasked as the anonymous Tory MP who penned a scathing *Observer* attack on Mrs T's 'A-level economics'. The outburst confirmed, at least in terms of a career in a Thatcherite Government, the MP's description of himself as 'unemployable'.

Freed from ambition for high office, and claiming to visit Aldershot only once a year, Mr Critchley has had time to polish his humorous lines in print and in Parliament. It was he who dubbed Mrs Thatcher 'The Great She Elephant' after an African ruler who considers the title a great honour. Our Premier is less impressed.

Neither can the Prime Minister have enjoyed another terse tribute from her rebel backbencher. 'The grander sort of Tory, faced with a tiresome woman, has long swapped her for another,' wrote Julian Critchley. 'But here it has been Mrs Thatcher who has been doing the swapping.'

Crossing the Floor

When an MP changes party allegiance, he or she is said to have 'crossed the floor' from the Government to the Opposition benches, or vice versa, in the Commons Chamber. It doesn't always happen literally.

Hardline Ulster Unionist Ian Paisley used to sit fairly happily with the Conservatives, as a legacy of the long alliance between the two groups. Then the Anglo-Irish Agreement led him to boycott Westminster in fury. When he returned it was with a new venom for the Tories. But he continues to sit on the Conservative side.

Some say, however, that it is immaterial where the member for North Antrim seats himself. If he spoke at his normal volume while reclining in the Commons car park, his voice would still carry into all corners of the Chamber.

Cuddly Toys

Lord Lyell, a Government Minister, is never lonely on his travels. He has long had his teddy bears Jimmy and Thumper for company. The cuddly creatures are likely to be dressed in clothes that match those of their master. And their safety is assured. When buying a new Porsche, the peer ordered special seat belts for his treasured toys.

Now Lord Lyell has confessed to growing out of such a childish pursuit. The toys are accompanied on his journeys by two more furry friends.

The peer's mother would find nothing odd in such bizarre behaviour. She has a doll, Griselda, whose wardrobe is also impressive.

Currie, Edwina

Some who talk through clenched teeth about That Woman mean this woman.

First noticed as a handcuff-waving speaker in a Conservative Party law and order debate, threatening to chain herself to a podium if her microphone was switched off, Mrs Currie has advanced with barely a pause for breath.

She has overcome the crippling shyness endemic to natives of Liverpool, and converted from Judaism to Anglicanism, to rise in Tory ranks. Despite her nickname of 'Cruella', she cares deeply about the eating habits of Northerners and the evils of smoking, though her boss and her husband – nicotine addicts both – have stubbed out her bid to ban the weed at work and in the home.

The public reacted with similar scorn to a suggestion from 'Vindaloo' that they should happily trade their second holiday in Spain for a day out with their dentist.

Said to have been regarded as a high-risk choice when appointed a Junior Health Minister, Mrs Currie herself had no such qualms, thoughtfully inviting the cameras to record her gracious acceptance speech when the promotion call came. She voted, of course, in favour of televising the Commons.

Energy, a thick skin and a sense of humour are keys to her success so far. Once asked whether she was upset at being dubbed 'Iron Tits', Edwina Currie replied: 'It doesn't worry me at all. I can enjoy sexual innuendo as much as the next man.'

Dalyell, Tam Champion questioner and old-Etonian maverick, Tam Dalyell (Labour, Linlithgow) is named after an ancestor who was the only man to escape from the Tower.

The current Dalyell helped sink Scottish devolution and has persistently raised the Belgrano episode of the Falklands War. The Left loved him until they remembered his liking for nuclear power.

Mr Dalyell sails on his singular way regardless of shifting allies and enemies.

Debate Once an MP has caught the Speaker's eye, he or she should be allowed to proceed in a speech without interruption. Except on a point of order. Or unless the debater is irrelevant, repetitive or out of order, in which case the Speaker should speedily intervene.

An MP in full flow may yield to an interruption for the purpose of explanation, but is entitled to refuse to give way.

Courtly rules have evolved in Parliament to cut down the chances of ugly confrontation. All speeches must be addressed to the Chair, and no MP may be directly referred to by name (*see* **Titles**). Similarly, to avoid criticism and a possible constitutional crisis, it was long a rule that Members of one House could not refer to the proceedings of the other during a debate. Now they get round it by talking about 'another place'.

A long list of banned insults has also been compiled in Erksine May, the Bible of Parliamentary procedure (*see* **Liar!**). No enemy or colleague in either House may be addressed as a red-necked rustiguts or slubberdegullion, for instance. And recently, Speaker Weatherill ruled that while 'wimp' was out of order in the Commons Chamber, 'wally' was acceptable.

The basic idea is that strength of reasoned argument should carry the day. But visitors often wonder how this worthy aim can be fulfilled when so many of the Parliamentary benches are deserted – until the division bell ushers in droves of Members to vote as their whips direct.

Deference The historic splendour and antique procedure of the Palace of Westminster are calculated to induce awe and respect among all those who enter its precincts. Sometimes undue deference results.

The tale is told, for instance, of a party of American tourists who were gazing in rapture at the opulent interior. Along came Lord Hailsham, gliding like a stately galleon in his Lord Chancellor's robes. The peer spotted an MP pal – Neil Marten – behind the visiting party. 'Neil!' he cried, with arms raised in greeting. The visiting party promptly dropped to their knees.

But some are uncowed by history. Take Mother Teresa for example. On a visit to London, to press Mrs Thatcher to 'do something' for the homeless, the saintly figure decided to walk from Parliament to Downing Street to plead her cause. Being led through Westminster Hall, she was invited by her guide to stop and admire the oldest and most splendid part of the Palace. 'Very nice', said Mother Teresa, as she surveyed the ancient structure. 'This would make an ideal night shelter.'

Democracy 'Democracy is the art of running a circus from the monkey cage.' (H. L. Mencken)

Deposits When lost amid a record crowd of election candidates during Finchley's declaration of 1983, Mrs Thatcher resolved that the election deposit – £150 since 1918 – should be upped sharply. Among the ten candidates ranged (or deranged) against her had been one standing on the Belgrano ticket. But any embarrassment caused was nothing to the humiliation of Jeremy Thorpe, at North Devon, in 1979. He was opposed by the writer Auberon Waugh, of the Dog Lovers' Party. (Remember a late lamented dog called Rinka?)

The £150 forfeited by candidates polling less than 12.5 per cent of the vote was judged by some self-publicists to be cheap at the price. One night-club owner in a northern city stood for election in a nearby prim and Methodist seat. His hostesses, drafted in as exotic canvassers, failed to convince the fiercely proper voters. But the businessman won valuable publicity for his bawdy bars.

Now the level of the election deposit has been raised to £500, and is lost by a candidate scoring less than five per cent of the vote. So only frivolous rich candidates remain in contention.

Despatch Boxes

If you should hear a Commons crowd crying 'Box! Box!' this is not an invitation for altercating members to fight out their grievances on *Grandstand*. It is simply that a Minister or leading figure from the Opposition, who is entitled to speak while standing beside one of the two despatch boxes on the Table of the House, has forgotten about this privilege. MPs like to keep things traditional.

The despatch boxes now in use – containing Bibles, New Testaments, the Hebrew Old Testament, and oath and affirmation cards for the swearing-in of new MPs – were post-war gifts from New Zealand. Already the Government box has been worn smooth at the corners after constant rubbing from sweaty ministerial palms.

The old despatch boxes, bearing the impressions of Gladstone's signet ring, received in moments of angry and impassioned oratory, were destroyed by bombs in 1941.

Disqualification

Aliens, bankrupts, and inmates of asylums, prisons or the House of Lords, are disqualified from voting or standing in Parliamentary elections.

Unless they happen to be Irish, when the logic of these rules is helpfully turned on its head. Citizens of the Republic are allowed to vote in UK elections and Irish peers can sit in the House of Commons, though not in the House of Lords.

Although there are purple peers – a 26-strong bench of bishops – in the Lords, neither clergy of the Churches of England, Scotland and Ireland nor Roman Catholic priests can sit in the Commons. Neither may anyone possessed of even the most missionary zeal participate if aged younger than 21 (voters must be 18).

Men and women who have not been caught in any of these disqualifying categories can still forfeit their seats if convicted of corrupt or illegal practices during their election campaigns. This is rare, however, as agents can usually be left to carry the can.

While a peer can behave with gentle eccentricity if so wishing – and indeed, may even be expected so do to – an MP should exercise more caution. For if medical experts identify insanity, which then does not recede after six months, a Member can be bundled from the green benches and into a white van.

Divine Right of Kings

Doctrine which held that a king derived his power direct from God and was therefore invested with an absolute right to override all other authorities.

Such an idea went to Charles I's head, causing him finally to lose it. The doctrine has latterly been replaced by the Divine Right of Prime Ministers.

Divisions All Parliamentary decisions are made by majority consent, either on the nod or by formal division into the voting lobbies.

When Members divide to walk into two voting lobbies, for or against a question, two tellers are appointed from each side. An 'Aye' teller and a 'No' teller stand together at each lobby exit, to avoid any possible (though doubtless accidental) discrepancies in the count.

The order 'Clear the Lobbies!' booms and then division bells ring out across Parliament, Whitehall and wired-up homes, restaurants and public houses within a mile or so radius of Westminster. Members have eight minutes to heed the call before the order 'Lock the doors!' is given. The entrances to the lobbies are then bolted, remaining so until the result of the division is announced.

Strangers are allowed to stay in the galleries during divisions, but not in the Members' Lobby. A ban was brought in after certain irate people affected by the result of a division tried to obstruct MPs on their way to vote.

MPs delaying arrival until the last seconds have occasionally charged into the wrong voting lobby. And there, once the door has slammed shut, they have had to remain, red-faced and the likely objects of ridicule by crueller opponents. The waiting-time is best used working out how the error can be explained to unforgiving whips.

Unfortunately for wrong-footed Members, news of the mistake does not end there. Division lists record the details of every vote, and are reproduced as official reports in *Hansard*. Journalists and pressure groups scrutinise each column of names closely and wayward Members may soon find that there is hell to pay in their constituencies.

Divisions are slightly different in the House of Lords, where the 'Ayes' and 'Noes' are dubbed 'Contents' and 'Not Contents'. Unlike the Speaker, the Lord Chancellor (or Lord Chairman) has an ordinary vote, which is taken in the House and not in the division lobby. This must have been a great relief for Lord Hailsham, who sat long on the woolsack and walked latterly with two sticks.

When a division is called, the order is given to 'Clear the Bar!' which may give some uninformed spectators the wrong impression of the dignified process. Peers then have just six minutes, or even less if the tellers agree, to traipse into the lobbies before the doors are locked. Which seems rather hard on tired old feet. Voting peers also get whacked (or at least tapped) with wooden wands carried by the tellers, who at the same time press a mechanical counter clutched in their other hand.

The conduct of a division, each one taking an average of more than ten minutes, eats into valuable Parliamentary time. The record is held by the radical People's Budget of 1909, which survived an exhausting 549 divisions.

These days there is periodic pressure for a new system of computer voting, allowing MPs to press button A or B and remain seated. But such calls for high-tech change never catch on.

Draftsmen Lawyers responsible for drafting Bills. Those located in the office of the Parliamentary Counsel to the Treasury handle government measures, while outside contractors are called in by MPs hoping to steer through legislation on private pet topics.

The job of legal eagles is to frame each Bill in correct Parliamentary language. As this is usually obscure and imprecise, the draftsmen tend to provide future work for legions of other lawyers.

Dress It isn't only Michael Foot, gracing the Cenotaph remembrance ceremony in his duffle coat, who has offended against the unwritten rules of proper political fashion. The sight of a Labour MP in cord trousers and open-necked shirt can cause much muttering among the grey-suited majority at Westminster, and even complaints to the Speaker. But the appearance of black Member Bernie Grant (Labour, Tottenham) in a kaftan during the State Opening of Parliament drew a diplomatic silence.

Parliament has always been ultra-conservative in its clothes sense. It drew the line at letting the Speaker and Serjeant at Arms wear trousers when they first became fashionable; even today these high officers continue to sport 18th-century court dress, featuring knee-breeches, jackets, lace frills and silver buckled shoes. And very fetching they look, too.

Any television cameras rolling in the Commons two centuries ago would have revealed a peacock Parliament with MPs clad in full court dress, complete with wigs and swords. County members would also have been entitled to wear spurs.

When Members were hatted in the Chamber, the convention arose that if anyone wanted to raise a point of order during a voting division, he or she had to remain 'seated and covered' – the easier to catch the Speaker's eye.

All went well until hats fell out of fashion. What then was to be done? Some undignified experiments followed. For instance, MPs draped their heads in handkerchiefs like certain seaside tourists, then sat under Order Papers. It was finally decided that the Serjeant at Arms should keep a hat in instant readiness. A senior MP presented him with a collapsible opera hat, which was also handy for storage.

In November 1979, the House having voted to retain the 'seated and covered' rule, the Speaker ordered that two hats should henceforth be available – one for each side of the House.

Most MPs do still like to dress for special occasions. Nicholas Fairbairn (Conservative, Perth and Kinross) may be unique in sporting capes and tartan trousers, but pride in appearance is widely spread. Among the proudest is Norman St John Stevas, now Lord St John of Fawsley, who once asked to be excused early from a Cabinet meeting because he had a lunch engagement to dress for.

'But Norman,' said a shocked Mrs Thatcher. 'I am also going to that function.'

'Yes Margaret, but it takes me much longer to change than it does you,' replied the Minister as he swept out.

Duels The mutual disdain between Mrs Thatcher and Mr Kinnock produces violent verbal duels, but so far they have refrained from a meeting with pistols at dawn. Unlike at least two of their predecessors.

Prime Minister Pitt (The Younger) asked, in May 1798, that a Bill to increase the Navy by 10,000 men pass all its stages in a single evening. As Britain was at war with France at the time, he claimed a national emergency. But the Opposition leader George Tierney denied that there was any special urgency.

'No man could oppose the Bill in the manner Mr Tierney has done,' replied Pitt, 'unless it were from a wish to impede the defence of the country.'

Fury erupted, but the Premier refused to withdraw his charge of virtual treason. A duel was demanded and accepted.

The pair met, with their seconds, at Putney Heath on the following Sunday afternoon. Each fired a single shot. Both missed by miles. Honour was held to have been satisfied.

Dukes The highest grade in the British peerage. A Duke is styled 'His Grace' and the 'Most Noble', unless officially addressed by the

Sovereign, when he becomes 'Our right trusty and right entirely beloved Cousin'. The latter, effusively friendly, greeting dates from the days when trust and love were often in short supply between monarch and nobility.

The honour is mostly inherited. But the Queen, when Princess Elizabeth, is said to have inquired of Winston Churchill, soon after he had led Britain to victory in the last war: 'Would you like a dukedom or something like that?'

Dunwoody, Gwyneth Broke battler for right-wing Labour causes and fur coats, Gwyneth Dunwoody (Labour, Crewe and Nantwich) sails close to the wind. Her seat is marginal, her finances terminal and her Shadow Cabinet career has been sunk by over-ambition.

The political commentator Andrew Alexander observed that she has 'all the charm and finesse of a sledgehammer'. Dennis Skinner put it even more cruelly. When Eric Heffer was making one of his periodic bids for the Labour leadership, he pleaded that politics should be considered above personalities. 'I know I'd come bottom in a beauty contest,' he said. 'You wouldn't if Gwyneth Dunwoody was standing,' piped up the Beast of Bolsover.

Dying on Duty

Stung by charges that Westminster – and especially the House of Lords – resembles a mortuary (when not a madhouse), Parliamentary managers have accepted an odd rule that no Member may die on the premises. It is designed to avoid unseemly inquests in a Royal palace.

There have, indeed, been several famous exits from the centre of power. Spencer Perceval achieved immortality by the manner of his going when, in 1812, he became the only British Prime Minister to be assassinated – shot dead by a lunatic in the lobby of the House of Commons. And, in 1979, Mrs Thatcher's trusted aide Airey Neave was blown up by an IRA bomb as he drove from the Commons car park.

But suddenly-deceased politicians are hurried from their offices, bars or the green or red benches of the debating Chambers, and rushed towards Westminster Hospital. They are later said officially to have breathed their last *en route*.

The macabre tale is told of one peer who remained seated after his colleagues had adjourned from their debate. When a flunky finally dared to try to rouse him from his slumbers, the noble lord was found to have been dead for several hours. So stiff was the corpse that bones had to be discreetly broken to ease him from his seat and into the nearby hospital. By such means are the dignity and rules of Parliament preserved!

Early Day Motion

Despite its hopeful-sounding title, this sort of motion rarely sees the light of day in the Commons Chamber.

It is set down for no specific day, and is thus described simply as a 'motion for an early day'. The aim of the exercise is to give certain views an airing, and sponsors often let their motions stand on the order paper to see how many signatures of support they attract. A heavily-backed Early Day Motion chides the Government that it should have thought of the matter first, and action may be prompted.

Electoral Register

A list of people qualified to vote at elections, which is drawn up by a Registration Officer in each constituency. If you don't return the form sent out each Autumn you could land in court facing a fine. And if you do fill it in you could also finish in court – giving jury service.

Besides being on display in your local library, the electoral list is also on sale to commercial outfits. So when you register to vote, you could in addition be signing up for a deluge of junk mail.

Emergency Adjournment Motions An MP can rise after Question Time from Monday to Thursday, and seek leave to move the adjournment of the House for the purpose of discussing 'a specific and important matter that should have urgent consideration'.

Whether the motion falls within the relevant Standing Order 9 is at the discretion of the Speaker who, if he agrees, will then ask Members who support the matter to rise. If 40 MPs think it worth the effort of jumping to their feet, the motion is assumed to have the backing of the House. If between 10 and 39 leap up, it is put to a vote. Should leave be given, the motion will be debated for up to three hours at the start of public business on the following day. Government whips then groan at the prospect of another all-night session.

What constitutes an emergency is a matter of considerable dispute. The motion is supposed to be based on fact not hearsay, and to raise a larger issue than a purely individual grievance. But MPs tend to raise all sorts of constituency problems under an emergency banner. It is worth their while even if ruled out of order, as they can expect good local media coverage of their valiant efforts.

Europe As we hurtle towards a truly Common Market in 1992, and Channel Tunnel burrowing digs deeper, many Britons are still unreconciled to life as Europeans. Some would still support Kenneth Tynan's sour condemnation of the EEC. 'I do not see the European Community as a great love affair,' the caustic critic explained. 'It is more like nine middle-aged couples with failing marriages meeting at a Brussels hotel for a group grope.'

The British seem rather uneasy in the European Parliament. Poor gropers, the Tories prefer to sit in a group consisting chiefly of themselves. Labour have long upset their strongly pro-EEC Socialist allies. And Les 'Gizzajob' Huckfield, that seasoned leftist seat-seeker, upset everyone when he unfurled a banner and bawled through a microphone during the miners' strike.

While some other Euro-MPs give the impression that their main aim is to devour as much of the EEC's food mountain as they can manage before draining the wine lake dry, Britons bicker among themselves. Suffolk Member Amadee Turner once said that he had long lived near to a nuclear power station and had suffered no ill-effect. 'Is that why you're so small?' quipped colleague Eric Forth.

E Exhibitionism

Exhibitionism All politicians are said to be exhibitionists, but a few elevate the habit into an art form – to the point that Westminster can boast some talented painters, who hold regular shows of their work inside the palace.

The former Tory Cabinet Minister, Lord Thorneycroft, is often seen sketching outside the Houses of Parliament, but the most talented artistic politician by far is Nicholas Ridley (Cirencester and Tewkesbury). The free-market Environment Minister is more used to being harried as a philistine than hailed as a gifted landscape painter. He remains the most famous survivor (after a certain Thatcher, Mrs M.) of those Tory MPs first elected in 1959 in what Rab Butler described as 'the worst intake of my experience'.

But soothing art bridges political divides. Each year MPs and peers, plus police officers and other Parliamentary staff, close ranks to display an often-acclaimed selection of their paintings.

Expenses Besides salaries, and possible fees as Parliamentary advisers, MPs have a wealth of allowances. Many are concerned with transport.

Car mileage rates for journeys within the triangle of House, home and constituency are graded in favour of grander, petrol-guzzling vehicles. An MP also collects travel vouchers – to swap for rail, sea or air tickets – for other official trips. Spouses and children of MPs are each allowed up to 15 free trips between home and House annually, so that they can refresh their memories of what their beloved politician looks like.

Previous Prime Ministers have carried a gold medallion entitling them to free rail travel anywhere in the UK. Mrs Thatcher has not needed hers, however. She has hardly ever let a train take the strain since she entered Downing Street.

Chauffeurs of ministerial limos also carry a medallion, which they show to police patrols when stopped for speeding, while the Minister sinks silently into the cushions on the back seat.

Use of an official car is a big bonus of political promotion (the Opposition leader gets one too). There are few sadder sights at Westminster than former Ministers queuing dejectedly for a taxi or bus, rueing the loss of the black limo that used to speed them home.

MPs get free stationery, inland telephone calls and postage from Parliament. They also draw secretarial and research allowances up to £21,302 a year for wages and general office expenses. Some MPs employ their wives as their secretaries. Love and devotion tend to be good excuses for paying a pittance.

In addition, Members with inner-London seats receive an annual payment of £1,023; and those with constituencies outside the capital can claim up to £8,107 each year for extra expenses incurred in staying overnight away from home.

MPs reluctantly retiring, and those ejected by their electors, have the consolation of an index-linked pension and generous severance pay. Members who have served less than ten years at Westminster can claim six months' salary and longer-servers are entitled to a full year's payment. Many of those exiting from the House of Commons also hope for speedy elevation to the House of Lords – where more allowances are available.

Fairbairn, Sir Nicholas

At the age of eleven, the young Scot Nicholas Fairbairn put out the windows of the Musselburgh Co-Op Bakery with his catapault on hearing of Labour's 1945 electoral victory. He has been firing verbal missiles in all directions ever since. Now Tory MP for Perth and Kinross, the gifted advocate and artist has nurtured the reputation of a passionate fop and a dandy. Mr Fairbairn once announced that he would be adopting frock coats in Parliament, to avoid a 'shiny bottom'.

Even in a profession where people tend to take themselves rather seriously, Mr Fairbairn stands out as self-obsessed. The first volume of his autobiography, *A Life Is Too Short**, contains the following first paragraph:

> Authors who want to be fashionable claim prodigious recollection of their earliest experiences. Anxious as I am to vie with them in that ambition, it would be taking a holiday from probity if I were to claim that I recall my conception. It was, I sense, unenjoyed and unintended by the half-consenting adults who were unsuspecting parties to it, and little can they have appreciated the pain which such a risk would cause for all concerned – especially me. But Priapus won the day – or rather the night. The skill which my male gamete demonstrated in slipping through the customs to improlificate my female component on that occasion created (in the mature zygote) an ineradicable urge to frustrate sterile authority at all times, and the pain which my conception caused to the keeper of the unsuspecting egg has ever since filled me with two resolves – to ingratiate myself in propitiation to the female species and to do all I could to frustrate unintended conceptions of my own.

Phew. It only goes to show that while a life may be too short, a life story can take far too long.

* Quartet Books

Fastest Results On the night of every General Election, a handful of seats vie to be the first to declare. In such divisions a recount would be considered a disaster. The record was set in 1959 at Billericay, which counted and announced the voters' verdict in just 57 minutes.

In 1987 Basildon and others were pipped for the honour by Torbay in Devon. There, Tory Rupert Allason (better known as spywriter Nigel West) was declared an easy winner after 61 minutes. 'This result has really put Torbay on the map,' said a delighted spokesman from the local tourist industry. 'We hope it will give a big boost to the local holiday trade.'

Sadly for Mr Allason, the spokesman was referring to the proven efficiency of counters from the borough council, not the expected benefits from a new and talented MP.

Father of the House Not the champion breeder in the House of Commons but the male MP who has put in the longest continual Parliamentary service, and who takes the chair during election of the Speaker. At present the honour is held by Sir Bernard Braine (Conservative, Castle Point), first of the intake of 1950 to take the oath of allegiance.

If there were such a thing as a Mother of the House, the title would go to a London housewife named Margaret Thatcher, last female survivor of the class of 1959.

Faulds, Andrew Booming-voiced actor Andrew Faulds (Labour, Warley East) is known for dramatic and irate interventions, if not for tact. He once savaged Norman St John Stevas for discussing abortion when 'he has not the capacity to put a bun in anyone's oven'.

Fawkes, Guy A folk hero who sought to set the Houses of Parliament alight during the reign of James I, and who ended up hung, drawn and quartered for his pains. Many new MPs, aiming to roast their more experienced enemies with fiery rhetoric, have finished up similarly crestfallen when their speeches flopped.

Curiously enough the name has also been adopted by a Tory dining club whose MP members are government loyalists unto death. Any fireworks they produce are certain to be damp squibs.

Fence Sitting A popular form of abuse for politicians who veer away from extremes, and who are accused of hedging their bets, is the claim that they are sitting on the fence. Hedges, fences, hurdles and divisions are, after all, the very stuff of party politics.

Most moderates are wary of the fence-sitting tag, fearing that it implies indecision. But not so Cyril Smith (SLD, Rochdale). The heavyweight MP, who once tipped the scales at a sturdy 29 stones, is proud of such a charge. 'If the fence is strong enough, I'll sit on it,' he thunders.

Feuds

British politics have seen some famous feuds between diehard opponents. One first-class war – now unfairly forgotten – was waged between the two Harolds, Macmillan and Wilson. 'If Mr Wilson went to school without his boots on it was because he was too big for them,' Supermac once drawled.

One of the finest, and longest-running feuds, was the Gladstone-Disraeli struggle which dominated much of Victorian politics. When asked to define the difference between 'misfortune' and 'calamity', the Tory showman offered: 'If Mr Gladstone fell into the Thames it would be a misfortune, but if someone pulled him out it would be a calamity.'

The 18th-century politician John Wilkes had a violent quarrel with the Earl of Sandwich for many years. Crossing paths by chance in a London club, the pair promptly crossed verbal swords as well. 'Sir,' stormed Sandwich, 'how will you die – of the pox or the gallows?'

To which Wilkes retorted: 'That, my Lord, depends on whether I embrace your mistress or your principles.'

Filibuster

A filibuster is an American word meaning a speech that runs on and on AND ON, with the aim of obstructing Parliamentary business by taking up as much time as possible.

The longest recorded continuous speech in the Commons Chamber was that of Henry Peter Brougham in 1828. He spoke for six hours on law reform. When he was created Lord Brougham and Vaux, he then set the House of Lords record in 1831, also for six hours, with his views on the Great Reform Bill. He admitted to being nobly 'fortified by three tumblers of spiced wine'.

Private Members' Bills are often talked out at Westminster. But otherwise, a standing order ruling against persistent 'irrelevance or tedious repetition' directs the Speaker or committee Chairman to order a verbose Member to sit down.

Labour MP for Newcastle-under-Lyme, John Golding spoke for a record eleven hours and fifteen minutes in committee on small amendments to the British Telecommunications Bill, on 8–9 February, 1983. His MP audience is unlikely to have appreciated such a marathon effort, but the relevant trade union did. Mr Golding became its leader.

Fire! The logical outcome of heated deliberations in the smoke-filled rooms of politics, perhaps. But the wealth of buckets, blankets and fire extinguishers around the Palace of Westminster underlines that it is a result to be avoided at all costs.

Once bitten twice shy, as the brides of Dracula might say. For the House of Commons was burnt down in 1834. The central heating system was overloaded with kindling which caught fire and destroyed almost all of the original Palace. Only Westminster Hall was saved intact – along, it is said, with Henry VIII's tennis balls which his lobs had left in the hammer beam roof three centuries earlier.

Conservationists of the day were horrified, but the disaster did produce the Gothic splendour (externally at least) of Sir Charles Barry's replacement Houses of Parliament. Still standing today, the building is known the world over – its image stamped on a million postcards and sauce bottles.

Fisticuffs A fair number of MPs have been invited to step outside the House of Commons after upsetting a pugilistic opponent, and a few punches have even been thrown within the hallowed Chamber.

On one occasion at least during the past century, there has been a mass brawl. When the Commons was sitting in committee to consider the Irish Home Rule Bill in 1893, logic gave way to a flurry of left hooks. In a throng of arguing MPs, the leader of the Irish Unionists struck a Nationalist Member with his clenched fist. The gesture was returned by another Republican and a free fight ensued.

Order was restored only when the Chairman of Committees sent for the much-respected Speaker Peel. But as the overwrought MPs returned to their places, it was said that the floor remained strewn with scarf-pins and false teeth.

Flattery Essential if an MP is serious about ascending the greasy pole of power politics. Cleverly congratulating a Minister on a typically dull speech may do more for the promotion chances of a new Member than long days of tedious toil on Commons committees.

A young hopeful in a hurry might find out what interests an influential figure. Let's say it happens to be greyhound racing. Here, for any newish MPs who may be reading, is the action plan: Bribe a tipster for a cert at the next Romford meeting (it may also help, of course, to know the man who wires the hare). Then when you bump into the great one in the Commons cafeteria, after hanging around for an hour or two, just slip this information into the vital seconds of ensuing chat. Providing the dog delivers, stand by for gratitude, affection and even a promotion call.

Mrs Thatcher, alas, has no time for gambling. So just as Irish Prime Minister Charles Haughey once charmed our leader at a sticky moment with a timely gift of antique silver, the Premier's favourites often say it with flowers.

All politicians like their achievements recognised. And when Mrs Thatcher invited batches of new MPs for cosy talks after the election, she expected thanks for engineering their victories. Most, but not all, obliged.

When the Premier asked one group of newcomers how their campaigns had fared, the first sensibly replied: 'Absolutely splendidly. And if we had only printed thousands of "I Love Maggie" stickers I would have doubled my majority.' Mrs Thatcher beamed.

Lulled by the good humour all about, the second MP said: 'I'm afraid my experience was rather different, Prime Minister. I found antagonism to you on the doorstep and I thought the national campaign left a lot to be desired.' The Prime Ministerial face became fixed, and the naive new boy found himself frozen out of the rest of the meeting. Indeed, no thaw is expected before the next election.

Fookes, Janet

This animal-lover and senior schoolmistress figure treats the committees she chairs like unruly classes. With a weakness for loud hats and turquoise outfits, Janet Fookes (Conservative, Plymouth Drake) was once mistaken for a Parisian tart.

One of her female predecessors in Plymouth, Nancy Astor, had a similar experience. During the war, when walking outside the House of Commons, she came across a Canadian seaman gazing with a baffled expression at the splendid edifice.

'Would you like to come inside, young man?' asked Lady A.

'Not likely,' the lad answered. 'You're the sort of dame my mother warned me about.'

Fooling

Abraham Lincoln's famous maxim, 'You can fool all the people some of the time, and some of the people all the time, but you cannot fool all the people all of the time', has been amended for modern usage.

The American humorist James Thurber offered, 'You can fool too many of the people too much of the time'.

And a current unofficial election motto savoured by Eric Forth MP (Conservative, Mid-Worcestershire) suggests, 'You can't fool all of the people all of the time – but do it just once and it lasts five years.'

Fowler, Norman

The timely exit of this wily, wiry Cabinet Minister as Secretary of State for Social Services is known in Whitehall as the Great Escape. Before moving to safer pastures, he used his time in the sensitive post to fight for the NHS – and broaden his education.

Persuaded to mount a frank public information campaign on Aids, Norman Fowler (Conservative, Sutton Coldfield) was typically thorough. He called a posse of experts together for a one-day conference so that he could be fully briefed on the complex and distressing condition.

The first speaker had barely begun a lecture on risky practices, when he was stopped by the Minister.

'What exactly is oral sex?' Mr Fowler asked. After being informed in some detail, the squeaky-clean Tory could only mutter 'Crikey.'

Freud, Sir Clement

Liberal gambler and former Fenland MP whose hangdog looks and monotone voice can baffle ally and opponent alike. As can his actions. . .

Sir Clement once invited colleague Cyril Smith to lunch at his posh club, and amazed the rotund Rochdale MP by selecting mouth-watering dishes for himself and not allowing his guest to order. Instead, Big Cyril was presented with a Lancashire meat and potato pie, followed by rice pudding. Confused and not a little embarrassed, he later recounted the tale to his mum.

'That's right,' replied the elderly Mrs Smith. 'Clement phoned yesterday and asked me what your favourite food was. So I told him.'

The writer, gourmet and former class winner of a *Daily Mail* London-New York air race wields a mighty wit. In one Commons debate, when an opponent fumed that violent criminals should get a taste of their own medicine, he murmured: 'What about rapists?'

Nursing a reputation for rudeness, he admits to strong dislikes. Firstly, cigarettes. A theatre manager once suffered a heart attack when attempting to end a row between the then MP and a defiant smoker. Secondly, anyone who wears Dr Scholl's sandals.

'I always feel that if people have something the matter with their feet it ought to be between them and their feet,' Sir Clement has explained. 'I very much mind being involved.'

His main regret is in having helped found the annual race to get the first bottle of Beaujolais Nouveau on to a London restaurant table, now arguing that the wine's quality is no longer worth all the fuss.

'We ought to start a competition to race it back to the vineyards,' he says.

Front Bench The front bench in the Commons Chamber as far as the centre gangway on the Government side (to the right of the Speaker) is occupied by Ministers. It is also called the Treasury Bench, though many of its occupants will be in concealed conflict with that penny-pinching department.

On the opposite front bench sit the leaders of the Opposition, or Shadow Cabinet.

At the foot of each bench runs a thin red line, beyond which MPs may not step. This is a safety device. The crimson markers are traditionally set two swords' lengths apart to

prevent an over-excited Member from pulling out a rapier and delivering a fatal jab into the person of a political enemy.

Conversely, the rank and file of Paliamentary parties are chiefly confined to the back benches of the Commons Chamber. And there, protected by their more exposed commanders, they aim verbal slings and arrows in safety – and plot an occasional stab in the odd colleague's back.

Fruits Those who visit Wimbledon solely to savour the strawberry teas may also include a trip to Westminster on their seasonal social circuit.

During the summer the doors of the Commons cafeteria open out on to a Thames-side terrace, where marquees are erected and strawberries served. MPs grin and bear the burden of offering a stream of supporters such a treat. Future campaign donations, canvassing and leaflet deliveries may depend on it.

Galbraith, Samuel Dr Sam Galbraith (Labour, Strathkelvin and Bearsden) is a House of Commons mould-breaker. He is Westminster's first brain surgeon – and may discover there much that merits his scalpel.

Gerry-mander Dividing electoral districts to benefit the party of power. The word recalls Governor Gerry of Massachusetts who, fearing for the public good if voters lost the benefits of his wisdom for another term, used this clever stratagem in 1812. It also refers to a certain sort of amphibian. . .

The story runs that while a group of politicians were studying an electoral map, one of them, commenting on the strange shape of a particular constituency, remarked: 'It looks like a salamander.' To which a colleague rejoined: 'You mean a gerrymander!'

The phrase stuck.

Gloucester, Duke of Royal males with seats in the House of Lords have largely stuck to platforms outside Parliament when making controversial comments.

Take Prince Philip, who once noted: 'To understand what Ministers are sometimes saying you must buy a gobbledegook dictionary and add an arbitrary ten years to every promise they make.'

But Prince Richard, Duke of Gloucester, is an exception. The bespectacled architect lit up the Lords with a maiden speech fuming against tobacco. He has been patron of the anti-smoking group ASH since his kinsman, Angus Ogilvy, decided to give up the post afte ccumbing once more to the wicked weed.

It is difficult to know what the Duke would have made of the Labour Minister who, on being offered a cigar by George VI, said: 'Oh, no thank you. I only smoke on special occasions.'

Gould, Bryan Had he stayed in his native New Zealand, whizzkid Bryan Gould might by now be in that country's Cabinet. Here, his chances look dicier. The architect of Socialist chic, Mr Gould is at least tipped as a possible successor to Neil Kinnock. In the meantime, he is not suffering too painfully for his beliefs. For much of the time he has represented depressed Dagenham, he's lived in style near hooray Henley.

Great Seal With a new design adopted at the start of each reign, the seal is still impressed on proclamations, writs, letters patent and documents giving power to sign and ratify treaties.

The office of the Lord Keeper of the Great Seal is now combined with that of the Lord Chancellor, and it is that title-holder's duty to keep the silver seal safe. This has at times brought problems.

In 1784, when the item had far more significance than it does today, Lord Chancellor Thurlow must have feared for his future when it was stolen from his home. Still, he could at least claim a royal precedent for such a loss. For a century earlier, James II had dropped the great seal into the Thames.

When Lord Chancellor, Lord Hailsham promised a young visitor to Westminster that good behaviour would be rewarded with a glimpse of the great seal. The child looked longingly towards the Thames throughout his stay, hoping to spot a great animal – perhaps performing tricks. He thought the silver disc poor consolation.

Greens A new title for the old Ecology Party, still championing conservation causes and offering a haven for devotees of wispy beards and sandals. Critics say the name refers to the naivety of the creed. But these days all the major parties claim to be green around the edges.

Griffiths, Sir Eldon No-nonsense MP (Conservative, Bury St Edmunds) and long-time Parliamentary adviser to the Police Federation, who once suffered the indignity of having his car stolen while he was dining with the boys in blue. To compound the felony further, the vehicle was then used as a getaway car by armed raiders before being recovered.

Guillotine The ultimate sanction against talkative politicians was popular under Robespierre and has been revived, in a rather less messy form, by modern Parliamentary business managers.

A guillotine is now a means of allocating time. It decrees that, after a given deadline, debate must stop. The drastic device is called on if a government feels harassed by delaying tactics from its opponents, or if fierce and disruptive debate is anticipated which jeopardises the programme for the session.

Erskine May says that 'It cannot be denied that they are capable of being used in such a way as to upset the balance, generally so carefully preserved, between the claims of business, and the rights of debate'. If so, the balance is being upset ever more frequently. Between 1921 and 1945, fourteen Bills were guillotined; 1945–75 saw thirty choppings; and 1976–May 1987 witnessed no fewer than forty-six.

Though guillotines cause cries of Opposition complaint, governments now regard them as a vital standby weapon. When the parties change places they reverse their arguments with no sign at all of any embarrassment.

Gummer, John Selwyn St John of Gummer (Conservative, Suffolk Coastal) succeeded Cecil Parkinson to the media-given title 'Cleanest Tory of Them All' and also followed him, briefly, as party chairman. This member of the Church of England Synod, popularly dubbed Seldom Glummer, summons most passion when bishop-bashing and when demanding that priests deal with moral rather than political matters. Whether this means that politics is an immoral pursuit is unclear.

According to one of his opponents, Mr Gummer – later reincarnated as an Agriculture Minister – has lent his name to the language. 'Well I'll be Gummered' is said to be a regular cry in rural areas. 'You can hear it in the cattle markets when a farmer discovers he's bid for a useless animal, or been undersold something,' the critic confides. . .

Handbagging A new verb – to handbag – has entered the political vocabulary.

Already the term is striking terror in the hearts of senior civil servants and Cabinet Ministers, not to mention a sizeable summit of European leaders. Even top military brass at the Ministry of Defence have received a series of handbaggings recently, usually for overshooting their spending targets.

The word has been coined by the Whitehall fraternity to denote a major carpeting from the Prime Minister. Not that Mrs Thatcher ever resorts to physical violence, of course. A verbal mugging is enough.

Hansard Official reports of Parliamentary debates, questions and division lists are named after the Hansard family whose firm originally published them.

They begin with brilliantly-skilled shorthand reporters sitting in the Press Gallery – who must be able to hear through the hubbub and have 200 words a minute at their fingertips. The reports are then written up, checked and edited, and are printed by Her Majesty's Stationery Office normally the day after the pearls of wisdom were first spoken.

Or almost spoken, perhaps. For *Hansard* is not a verbatim report. Grammar is corrected and superfluous repetition struck out. Ums and ers are axed, with the result that the poorest speaker is made to sound as eloquent as the master orator.

Most Parliamentary sittings see a steady flow of MPs dashing to the *Hansard* office half an hour after finishing their speeches, hoping to 'correct' the manuscript before it is sent to the printers. The editor's word is final, but the appeal of the anxious MP who has bungled a particular phrase or point usually finds a sympathetic ear.

Hattersley, Roy Roy Hattersley has had to cut his political coat to suit his cloth to survive as Labour's deputy leader – while lately having to let out his garments substantially around the waistline.

Dubbed by David Owen 'the acceptable face of opportunism', Mr Hattersley (Birmingham Sparkbrook) has veered to the left while remaining firmly committed to the good life. A prolific writer, he has turned his attention from journalism to novels. One possible Hattersley hero is a nostalgic Yorkshire exile, hooked on cricket, Sheffield Wednesday and Hovis adverts, who wheels and deals to stay ahead in politics, pausing only to partake of some sumptuous meals. Fact, as they say, is stranger than fiction.

Hatton, Derek

Former boss of Liverpool city council for three and a half turbulent years from May 1983. This was a period in which the council teetered on the brink of bankruptcy, and officials were once despatched in a taxi to deliver redundancy notices to the entire council workforce. And such were the tragi-comic capers enacted in the council chamber that the local paper sent its drama correspondent to cover them.

Mr Hatton was finally ejected from his city hall seat for failing to set a rate, and expelled from the Labour Party as part of the purge on Militant. Telling his side of the story in a typically self-effacing autobiography, he said: 'My biggest asset was my mouth'. Not quite. His head and his ego are larger still.

Having accepted a series of modelling assignments not normally taken by class-war Trotskyists, sharp-suited Derek is now involved in another form of personal presentation. He has got into public relations, and will probably make a fortune from it.

Healey, Denis

One failed American Presidential candidate needed costly opinion polls to find out why, after putting his case so lucidly, he hadn't won the voters' trust. A lack of eyebrows was found to be to blame. Though the politician belatedly began to pencil some in, the damage was done. On such a test of stature, of course, Denis Healey would have been unbeatable.

The Leeds East MP has bullied and bulldozed his way through the higher offices of state and is still regarded by many as the best leader Labour never had.

His merciless wit has made life miserable for his enemies. He once said that being attacked by his then opposite number, Sir Geoffrey Howe (Conservative, East Surrey), was like being 'savaged by a dead sheep'. Mr Healey later corrected himself. It was like being 'nibbled by a hearth-rug'.

Neither has the Prime Minister escaped Mr Healey's withering scorn. Nicknames like 'Bargain Basement Boadicea', 'Rhoda the Rhino' and 'Attila the Hen' are all his work.

Stepping from the aircraft on a crucial visit to Moscow, Mr Healey was quick to relax a tense situation. Surveying his Kremlin welcoming committee he boomed, 'I see it's the same old Mafia.'

'Hear! Hear!' This, rather than vulgar handclapping, is the traditional Parliamentary expression for applauding a speech. It is an abbreviation of 'Hear him! Hear him!', which was popular at political gatherings at the start of the 19th century. The trouble is, with so much heckling and barracking these days, Members often can't. Or won't.

The phrase is not to be confused with the ironic 'Ha! Ha!' which, from certain throats, can be stretched into four or more syllables. Neither should it be mistaken for the frequently heard 'Haaarrgghhh!' This covers a multitude of meanings from 'You blithering idiot!' to 'My God, I should never have had those garlic prawns for lunch'.

Sometimes the wise are silent. Clever politicians have probably heard the tale of the 18th-century playwright and MP Richard Brinsley Sheridan, who led his intended victim into a brilliant trap through his denunciation of another. 'Where, oh where, shall we find a more foolish knave or a more knavish fool than this?' Sheridan asked the House.

At which the unfortunate Member identified himself with a rash cry of 'Hear! Hear!'

Heckling Time was when every campaign was dominated by the public meeting. Halls and market squares would be packed with people eager for information, entertainment and perhaps a lively exchange of views. For here the noble art of humorous heckling was honed. Only the sharpest politicians remained unscathed.

One survivor was Nancy Astor, the first woman to take a Commons seat, who fenced with hecklers throughout her long political career. At one early meeting, she faced a barrage from a hostile farmworker, who felt that such a sophisticate must be ignorant of rural life.

'How many toes are there on a pig's foot?' he bawled.

'Take your boots off and show us,' came the reply.

At another gathering, a heckler shouted out: 'Your husband's a millionaire, ain't he?'

'I should certainly hope so,' returned Lady Astor. 'That's why I married him.'

And once a working-class mother shouted out during an Astor address: 'My children are as good as yourn!'

'As which of mine?' asked Lady A. swiftly. 'I've got some worse than any of yours – but I might have one who was better.'

Sadly, with the advent of television, most people expect to be entertained at home. Rare is the studio audience that revives the clever craft of quickfire repartee. And rare too is the spontaneously witty politician.

Heffer, Eric High Anglican Marxist Eric Heffer (Labour, Liverpool Walton) is a class war warrior who never knows when he is beaten. Except on one occasion when he was attending a meeting of Labour's National Executive Committee, and sought to storm out in protest at a certain revisionary plan.

The first door he pulled open turned out to be a broom cupboard. So did the second. Cursing loudly, Mr Heffer decided that it was easier to stay put.

This proud proletarian has an original line of attack. He has accused the Tories of being 'a load of kippers – two-faced with no guts.' But he has also fallen victim to his own fury.

Having elegantly condemned Michael Heseltine for messing with the Mace, he saw nothing wrong in defending left-winger Ron Brown from punishment over an even more damaging charge a decade later. 'This is using a sledgehammer to crack a . . .' he began.

By the time the awful double meaning of his words had dawned it was too late. MPs had burst into laughter.

Heseltine, Michael Millionaire Michael Heseltine (Conservative, Henley) remains the darling of the Tory conference and a favourite to follow Herself, despite their dramatic parting of the ways over Westland. He combines David Owen's twin virtues of being 'tough and tender', earning the nicknames Goldilocks and Tarzan. Though the Young Conservatives are bursting with Heseltinies, staider souls regard him as being a little too reckless (*see* **The Mace**)

Soon after bailing out of the Cabinet, Mr Heseltine was spotted between lines of exhibition blooms at the Westminster Rose Show. He stopped at every vase and name tag, and smelt each scent in turn. Until he came to a modest little flower labelled 'Margaret Thatcher'. The ex-Minister walked quickly on, without so much as a sniff.

Hurd, Douglas Perfect gent and past career diplomat Douglas Hurd (Conservative, Witney) is a survivor of the lions' den – the Tory Conference at which, as Home Secretary, he bravely resists the return of the rack and the rope almost annually.

Despite his understated views, Mr Hurd has a very vivid imagination, which he has put into print. He has so far penned such classics as *The Truth Game*, *Vote To Kill* and *An End To Promises* – not the titles of Tory manifestoes, but of political thrillers to rival the writings of Jeffrey Archer. Indeed, one Hurd volume dealt with an imaginary civil war between northern and southern Britain.

Labour alleges that, as Conservative rule continues, the idea is fast taking root.

Incon-venience 'Half the doors (in the House of Commons) that have no labels on them turn out to be men's lavatories, but nobody tells you that,' says Tory Teresa Gorman of Billericay. She obviously found out the hard way.

Indepen-dent Few people who take no party whip, and who are free to exercise their own judgment, have been elected to Parliament since the abolition of the university seats in 1950. They hang on as Crossbenchers in the unelected House of Lords.

Independents still survive in rural local government, but even here they are in decline. All parties claim to mourn their passing, while merrily whipping their own Members as often as possible.

The last elected Independent MP was Ulster's Frank Maguire, a Republican publican from Fermanagh and South Tyrone. He rarely bothered to make the journey over the Irish Sea to Westminster; but he did once appear, in the dying days of the Callaghan Government, for a crucial and closely-fought vote.

Labour whips pleaded with him to pass through their voting lobby. But Mr Maguire would not be moved from his seat. 'I am here to abstain in person,' he informed apoplectic MPs, and resolutely stayed put.

The Government then lost the vote by 311 to 310, and fell from power.

Intelligence The secret (sic) variety works from the shadowy recesses of Whitehall. But the sort that may involve a deficiency in IQ counts shows itself more visibly. Vocally, too. As Winston Churchill – ever the master of the comic put-down – bemoaned in the following Question Time exchange:

> **Mr Lewis (Labour):** Is the Prime Minister aware of the deep concern felt by the people of this country at the whole question of the Korean conflict?

> **Churchill:** I am fully aware of the deep concern felt by the Honourable Member in many matters above his comprehension.

Jam

Displaying underrated flashes of humour, former Premier Edward Heath (Conservative, Old Bexley and Sidcup) has occasionally delivered a decent pun. From the Opposition Front Bench he was once laying into the Minister of Transport. A noteless speaker, the then top Tory continued: 'He has done nothing to alleviate our traffic problems. But he is the only Minister who produces jam today as well as promising jam tomorrow.'

Jargon

A growth industry in Westminster and Whitehall. Winston Churchill once mocked a tortured and confusing piece of officialese with the phrase: 'This is the sort of English up with which I will not put.' But the irony seems to have been ignored, as the flow of wordage has since turned into a flood.

How far we are from the primitive days of ancient Egypt, when a Minister could send a note to a senior civil servant, simply saying: 'Appollonius to Zeno, greeting. You did right to send the chickpeas to Memphis. Farewell.' Now officials in London and Brussels would need to fell a small forest to pen a reply.

Periodic assaults are made on gobbledegook and guff. Writing a foreword to a recent *Making it Plain* booklet appealing for concise language in the civil service, Mrs Thatcher attacked the use of pompous words, long sentences and endless paragraphs in official papers. 'It is no exaggeration to describe plain English as a fundamental tool of good government,' she declared.

If you want that in simple language, 'Plain English is a fundamental tool of good government.'

Jenkins, Lord (Roy)

Urbane historian Lord Jenkins of Hillhead, now Chancellor of Oxford University and leader of the Social and Liberal Democratic peers, seems in manner the model of a conservative country gent. But he is a miner's son and a sporadic radical.

Taking the strange ridicule of the peer's legendary fondness for fine wine a little further, one commentator said Roy Jenkins was 'not built for the death fast, but for the slow lunch'.

Clean-up campaigner Mary Whitehouse disagrees. She notes that the politician steered through a welter of liberal legislation while Home Secretary in the late 1960s, and on his Jiminy Cricket-like head she slams the label 'architect of the permissive society'.

Johnson, Dr Samuel Among Samuel Johnson's lesser-known works are reports of Parliamentary debates, which appeared in *The Gentleman's Magazine* during the 1740s. Never visiting the public gallery himself, he rewrote speeches in a way that was said by some to bear little or no relation to the actual words spoken.

As reports of Parliament were a breach of privilege in Dr Johnson's day, the author could claim that he was justified in using his imagination. His publishers used anagrams of actual MPs' names, and headlined the debates as hailing from the 'Senate of Lilliput'.

An avowed Tory, he made no effort to conceal his bias. 'I took good care that the Whig dogs should not have the best of it,' the good doctor once remarked.

So began a strain of partisan political journalism which is still popular today. . .

Samuel Johnson might particularly have approved of the masthead to *The Sporting Times*, which carried the legend 'High Toryism, High Churchism, High Farming and old Port forever'.

Jollies MPs who have not upset their whips too often, and who have settled in at Westminster, can look forward to a couple of 'jollies' – trips abroad – each year. So get elected, and see the world.

Most jollies last for four or five days, but giant freebies lasting an entire month are not unknown. Fact-finding parties will be drawn equally from both sides of the House of Commons. An unpaired Member may be summoned home by the Whips at any time, but if a crisis vote occurs the whole party will be ordered to return.

The best way an MP can get about a bit is by joining a Select Committee. Most undertake regular surveys of relevant innovations and practices in foreign countries. There is usually time on such occasions for some tourist-style sight-seeing as well. Most popular is the Defence Select Committee, whose members traverse the globe at least once a year carrying out doubtless desperately-crucial reviews of our bases abroad.

Other ways of landing a jolly are by joining an All-Party Committee specialising in a certain country. So you might get to study tensions in Sri Lanka at first hand – and, take heart,

away from the trouble spots the island is still a holiday paradise! Or MPs with wanderlust might enlist in the Inter-Parliamentary Union or the Commonwealth Parliamentary Associations, all of which often ferry restless politicians to and fro.

Kennedy, Charles Tipped to be the likely leader of the Social and Liberal Democrats long before he reaches his 40th birthday, Charles Kennedy (Ross, Cromarty and Skye) shared the general amazement at his first electoral victory in 1983. After an enjoyable campaign in the glorious Highland seat, he expected to return to his political studies at Indiana University.

Having won the country's largest constituency, however, he had to switch swiftly from theory to practice.

Although able to get the better of his formidable former party leader David Owen, during the machinations over the Alliance merger, Mr Kennedy has had to admit defeat in other campaigns. Despite several valiant bids to forsake tobacco, he remains a martyr to the weed. Such are the pressures of centre party politics, that nicotine is needed for fraying nerves.

Kinnock, Neil

Opinion is split on whether Labour leader Neil Kinnock (Islwyn) is a Welsh wizard or windbag. Critics might echo Winston Churchill's description of Ramsay MacDonald: 'We know that he had, more than any other man, the gift of compressing the largest amount of words into the smallest amount of thought,' said the Tory titan. And in partial support of such a theory, the verbose Mr Kinnock sports an almost permanently inflamed larynx.

Friends counter that the Socialist supremo is the best-read of our party leaders (Mrs Thatcher rarely opens a book, though she did once admit to 're-reading' a Frederick Forsyth thriller) and that he takes after his heroes Michael Foot and Nye Bevan as a warm and witty orator.

Aided by Tracey Ullman, Hugh (*Chariots of Fire*) Hudson and a horde of trendy PR consultants, the Welshman turned from a welter of words to a 1987 American-style election campaign based on image.

For the launch of the grand performance, a London hall was packed with waiting journalists and TV cameras. Suddenly stirring music played, lights blazed and down the aisle strode Mr Kinnock and his deputy, Roy Hattersley.

Doubtless a neat idea on paper, said satirist Michael White. In practice, however, it looked like a gay wedding.

Knives

Shirley Williams was having trouble working a flick knife at a Liberal-SDP Alliance Press conference on law and order.

Turning to Dr Owen, the SDP leader, she said: 'David, I believe you know how to use one of these.' It was a significant joke.

Lavatory Humour

A persisting legacy of the public school system which has sent so many of its old boys to Westminster.

Best practitioner of the art was Winston Churchill. When Churchill was Prime Minister, Clement Attlee was once using a Commons urinal. The PM entered, then moved as far away from the Labour leader as possible.

'Standoffish today, aren't you Winston?' Attlee inquired.

'Yes,' replied Churchill. 'Show a Socialist something strong and successful and he will try to grab it.'

And when, in his final years of high office, Churchill was told on leaving a loo that his flies were undone, he remained unfussed. 'It is a fact well known that a dead bird never falls from its nest,' the great man muttered.

Lawson, Nigel An ex motor torpedo boat captain in the Royal Navy, Nigel Lawson (Conservative, Blaby) has continued to operate on similar lines in Parliament. Labour loathes him (*see* **Banks, Tony**). He is the long-serving Chancellor who dared to fire shots at Mrs Thatcher over exchange rates, and who was not sunk in return. He is noted, too, for the mountainous plates of food he consumes in the Commons canteen.

Weeks after the 1988 Budget, Mrs Thatcher finally acted to end speculation of a spat with her Chancellor. She gave Mr Lawson, her next-door neighbour in Downing Street, the keys to the 45-bedroom Buckinghamshire mansion of Dorneywood – which is conveniently near to her own official country residence of Chequers.

It may have been a reward for loyal service . . . or it may have been a ploy to keep a wayward Chancellor always close at hand!

'Liar!' This is a word you are not supposed to hear in Parliamentary debates, where it is an offence to impugn a Member's honesty or integrity.

But clever MPs have long found ingenious ways to break the ban. When Richard Brinsley Sheridan was called to order two centuries ago, for making just such a charge, he replied: 'Mr Speaker, Sir. I said that the Honourable Gentleman was a liar it is true and I am sorry for it.'

He added that the Honourable Member could put the punctuation marks where he wished.

Library Fronting the Thames in the House of Commons, this six-room suite is the place where MPs come to mug up or wind down.

It boasts some 160,000 volumes and subscribes to 1,700 periodicals and more than 100 newspapers. Ladies with scissors snip each day away compiling cuttings files on every conceivable topic; and a team of researchers is dedicated to giving MPs the fullest and speediest brief for their latest assaults on the Government.

Clearly the helpful staff have come to ignore the advice given in the 1774 *Old Librarian Almanack*, which ran: 'Let no Politician be in your Library, nor no man who Talks overmuch. It will be difficult for him to observe Silence, and he is objectionable otherwise, as well.'

There should be little noise from the crowd of MPs sitting at the library desks who are engrossed in their mail or in preparing an article, question or speech. The inkwells are always kept filled for a single Member who continues to work with a nib, so there could be a faint scratching sound from a lone Parliamentary pen.

The main disturbance is likely to come from armchairs ranged around the fireplace, and takes the form of unmistakable snores. From early afternoon MPs tired after late-night sessions, morning committees or long lunches are to be found asleep in these relaxing surroundings.

Most will try not to advertise the fact. One MP, however, serves notice that he is about to be out for the count by taking off his glasses, placing a white handkerchief over his face and then putting his glasses on again.

Lines

A politician's life runs on a number of lines. First are the sort in speeches which must not be fluffed. And second are the whips' underlinings that must not be miscounted . . .

On Thursday evening, soon after the Parliamentary business for the ensuing week has been announced, every Member is sent by his or her party whips' office a circular – also called, rather confusingly, a 'whip' – which shows by underlinings the relative importance given to each item.

One line means the Member can safely stay away for the day, as no vital votes are due. Two lines mean that attendance is expected unless the MP is 'paired' with a Member of the Opposition, when both can be absent. But a three-line whip means that an appearance is essential.

If an MP misses a three-liner the whips will want to know why. Only serious illness or family bereavement is accepted as a valid excuse.

Otherwise, the missing Member can expect a verbal lashing and a black mark against future promotion.

Livingstone, Ken

Westminster has contained some ghostly apparitions who drift through its corridors, bereft of their own office space. One such was Ken Livingstone (Labour, Brent East). But he got fed up with drifting around Parliament 'like some kind of medieval ghost' untethered to desk or telephone, and went home to his newts in a huff.

Though the former leader of the Greater London Council had tried direct action (commandeering an empty room one day, only to find it padlocked the next) he did not help himself in other ways. His outbursts on Ulster and on colleagues who, he said, haunted bars and brothels, enraged the Labour whips.

Which was not wise, for they allocate office space – and they shut Red Ken out.

Labour leaders may also have been mindful of the fate that befell moderates who steered the Socialists to victory in what was to prove the last GLC-wide elections. The very next day, Mr Livingstone pulled off a classic coup. The saga inspired Frederick Forsyth to write *The Fourth Protocol*, in which a Labour government is felled by the Left.

However, Ken Livingstone is not alone in feeling bereft in the cramped and crowded House of Commons. Some MPs have had to wait several years before being allocated a desk. While self-denial is a virtue, such official stinginess is surely a sin. Voters are the victims.

Lobby Correspondents

Lobby (or political) correspondents are a select band of Parliamentary journalists, drawn from the ranks of the Press Gallery, who provide the background to what's going on at Westminster. They are allowed direct contact with MPs in the Members' Lobby, and work to the strict principle that their sources are never revealed (even on pain of prison).

So a leak which is attributed to 'reliable sources' or 'sources close to the Minister' may mean the relevant Minister himself.

And although the Prime Minister may fume at the recent flood of unwanted leaks, Downing Street itself is anything but watertight. Lobby journalists have regular briefings with the Premier's mouthpiece, Bernard Ingham, whose every utterance has been cleared by Herself. But, officially, such meetings never occur.

The mutual dependency between journalists and politicians sees an inevitable fraying of tempers at times and, alas on rarer occasions, some brilliant humour.

A former chairman of the Press Gallery is fondly remembered for a reply to a lunchtime speaker who ranted and raved against the Press. In the course of a long diatribe, the critic had referred to the 'Taily Delegraph'. Moving the vote of thanks, the quick-thinking chairman said that ever since hearing a BBC radio announcer mention the 'Fome and Horses Programme', he had been wary of Spoonerisms.

'For that reason I would never describe anybody as a shining wit,' he concluded. 'Least of all our speaker.'

Lobby Fodder

MPs are always being asked to send their favourite recipe to some sort of charitable publication or other. Secretaries normally keep a stock of various mouthwatering choices – sometimes made up by themselves, it is rumoured – to ensure variety.

One of the most humorous, dubbed Lobby Fodder, comes from the Social and Liberal Democratic peer Lord Tanlaw. It runs as follows:

A quick-meal recipe for Parliamentarians in a hurry and on a tight budget. No previous culinary expertise necessary.

two slices wholemeal bread
one egg
Four pats 'airline' butter (not margarine), or one inch cut from 250g pkt.

Beat egg in a basin.
Drop in bread and soak both sides.
Melt butter in frying pan.
Add bread to frying pan.
Fry each side for about 30 seconds; do not burn, then serve.

Plus points:
1. quick and easy – five mins. approx. for preparation, cooking and consumption;
2. cheap – 10p approx. excluding the butter; this should be saved from in-flight meals or Members' dining rooms;
3. sustaining, with high protein value;
4. absorbs alcohol well.

Minus points:
1. edible rather than tasty;
2. lady companions do not respond well when served Lobby Fodder in lieu of dinner at Lockets;
3. high cholesterol content could induce an unexpected by-election.

Lobbying Literally the practice of entering the lobby of the Houses of Parliament to influence Members' votes on some proposed legislation. All electors have a right to get into Westminster and demand to see their MP, but some will inevitably be displeased with the warmth of their reception.

A few miffed and militant protesters have resorted to on-site direct action. In recent times abuse, horse dung, pots of paint and showers of leaflets have all been hurled down from the public galleries in the Commons Chamber on to surprised MPs below.

Even the dignity of the House of Lords has been jolted by sudden outbursts from normally silent spectators. Long before a band of lesbians abseiled down to the floor of the Upper House, the actress Vivien Leigh – who had been seated in Black Rod's guest box – rose up and delivered an emotional address against the planned demolition of the St James's Theatre.

As shock waves resounded through the Chamber, Black Rod leant forward and whispered to the actress 'You'll have to go now'. She apparently thought he had said 'You have a go now' and was spurred on in her speech. Doorkeepers finally bustled her out.

In recent years lobbying has become a professional and discreet multi-million-pound business. But in these days of guaranteed Government majorities, paid lobbyists are more likely to approach Ministers or senior civil servants direct – and give humble backbenchers in the House of Commons a miss.

Lord Chamberlain

This post is not to be confused with that of the Lord Great Chamberlain, a shared hereditary office which was nominally the chief authority over the Palace of Westminster until 1965.

The Lord Chamberlain is appointed by the Government as the chief officer of the Royal Household. He, too, lost his most interesting duties in the 1960s, for he was formerly responsible for the licensing of plays for public performance.

Thus the Lord Chamberlain used to read more pornographic literature than Lord Longford, Mary Whitehouse and five old men in dirty raincoats put together.

Lord Chancellor

The office of the Lord High Chancellor of Great Britain and Keeper of the Great Seal is the most historic and dignified under the Crown. However, Lord Hailsham, a previous holder of the post, has admitted that he amused himself by quietly muttering expletives at the bishops' benches during lordly but long-winded debates.

Such personages have wielded, on occasions during the last 900 years, power only slightly less than that of the monarch. The Lord Chancellor still takes precedence, after the Royal Family, over all Her Majesty's subjects except the Archbishop of Canterbury. Killing the Lord Chancellor is high treason.

Any Prime Minister who feels that salary is the surest sign of status might have cause to resent this particular colleague. For while Mrs Thatcher was entitled to £62,698 in 1988 (and drew only £51,068), Lord Mackay – the present Lord Chancellor – received a princely £83,448.

The Lord Chancellor is appointed by the Government, sits in the Cabinet and cannot be a Roman Catholic. He is a weaker Speaker in the Upper House, wielding less power than his House of Commons colleague – the well-behaved peers police themselves – and head of the entire legal system in England and Wales.

Thus – perhaps as a sign of how real power has shifted down the centuries – the office that was once held by a top cleric is now filled by a leading lawyer.

Lords of Appeal

Law Lords are legal eagles of great experience who sit in the UK's highest court, the House of Lords. Their function is not to give a judgement but to clarify the law and give a considered opinion regarding an appeal.

As with other deliberations at Westminster, expert opinion is sometimes divided.

Lords Spiritual

As opposed to the secular Lords Temporal. Before the suppression of the monasteries by Henry VIII in 1539, priors, abbots and bishops filled more House of Lords benches than did their lay brethren.

These days there are just 26 peers in purple – two Archbishops and 24 senior bishops – who take no party whip and who frequently disagree, with great gentility, among themselves.

Time was when such clerics were of vital importance. With the religious houses long England's sole centres of learning, they were often the only peers who could read and write. Deciphering official documents could thus be difficult without their help.

So monarchs would send for church chiefs selectively when they needed to know the news – favouring those of great scholarship and, perhaps, of great wealth. Both could be put into the service of Crown and country.

Now that the joys of literacy have spread into most corners of Westminster, the bishops are merely 26 among a clued-up lordly crowd nearly 900-strong. But they have kept to themselves the privilege of leading, on a rota system, the prayers which begin each sitting.

Lowest Vote

Standing for the Yorkshire seat of Ripon in 1860, Temperance Chartist hopeful F.R. Lees won no votes at all. The public houses for miles around were filled with thirsty crowds toasting the only recorded nil vote in British electoral history. Even the candidate – if able to vote – was not convinced of his own qualities, it seems.

Since universal franchise, the lowest popularity rating at the polls has gone to Lieutenant Commander William Boaks (Public Safety Democratic Monarchist White Resident). The cranky commander spent many happy and unfruitful years, plus a small fortune in lost deposits, touring the land and raising his banner at by-elections.

Meeting massive indifference everywhere, he notched up the lowest vote at Glasgow Hillhead in 1982 when only five voters thought that the institution to which he should be sent was the House of Commons.

M0, M1, M2, M3 Nightmare definitions of the amount of money in the economy, which give politicians who are supposed to know about such things sleepless nights.

Do not feel uninformed. Many MPs don't understand the differing terms, either. Indeed, rumour has it that all four titles are regularly mistaken for motorways (with M0 perhaps standing for the M25 during rush hour standstills).

Economics has floored some of our most high-flying political talents. After all, it's far easier to make glorious spending plans than to work out how you are going to pay for them.

The problem once taxed Willie Whitelaw, when he was challenging Mrs Thatcher for the leadership of the Conservative Party. His campaign managers realised that their man was no economic whizz. 'At least pretend to know about M3,' they told him.

The standard-bearer obliged. He was seen being interviewed on television by David Dimbleby, who asked a complex and seemingly unending question on monetary policy.

Willie Whitelaw waited amiably for the flow of words to stop, then managed a sharp and decisive reply.

'Yes,' he said.

The Mace Once a great club for the battering-in of heads, the Mace now has a purely ceremonial function.

As a symbol of the authority of the Speaker and of Parliament, the Mace is placed on the Table of the House when the Commons is sitting – along with two despatch boxes, assorted books, water bottles and fancy stationery. When the House moves into committee, it is placed under the Table.

The object has assumed a vital role during tense points of history. Charles I tried to suspend Parliament by sending for the Mace. Not surprisingly, MPs refused to part with it.

A few years later Cromwell called in soldiers to clear the House, and eject the Speaker from the Chair. By ordering the removal of the Mace (which he dubbed 'this bauble') he actually established even more fully that Parliament could not sit without it. This is one of many examples in political history, where actions have had the opposite results to those intended.

MPs have several times wrestled over possession of the Mace.

In the late 1970s Tory MP Michael Heseltine earned the nickname 'Tarzan' after swinging the object around his head and threatening to use it for its original purpose. Friends restrained him.

Then Labour left-winger Ron Brown damaged the Mace by dropping it to the floor. Wits said that the object ended up like the MP – cracked. But there was little amusement at Mr Brown's scornful apology ('grovel grovel'). He said, 'I do not justify what I did. Dropping the damn thing was a mistake. I should have taken it home with me, raffled it and got some money for the National Health Service.'

Such humour saw the MP suspended from Parliament and from the Labour whip.

The House of Lords also uses a Mace, but peers are far less likely to resort to violence over it. Lord Simonds, a formidable Lord Chancellor from the 1960s, held the Mace in particular respect – even imagining that it had a personality of its own. He admonished a new peer, who had broken a House rule by crossing the floor between the Woolsack and the Table, with the words: 'Never do that again, I beg of you. I don't mind at all but the Mace simply hates it.'

Maclennan, Robert

Robert Maclennan (SLD, Caithness and Sutherland) proved a tough backroom negotiator during painful talks on Alliance merger.

In public, however, he seems to vanish beneath his loudly-checked suits. Indeed, it has been said that the Scottish barrister is Britain's only politician to have had a completely successful charisma bypass.

Madness

'We shape our buildings and afterwards our buildings shape us,' said Winston Churchill. It was unfortunate, therefore, that the designer of the Palace of Westminster, Augustus Pugin, was dragged off to a lunatic asylum soon afterwards.

Tales of insanity among the inmates of the Palace of Westminster are legion, especially within the elevated ranks of the House of Lords. Several peers have had their own keepers.

Some Members have gone off their heads quietly and rather charmingly. Others have made a great fuss.

In 1841, for a motion of no confidence in the Government, Opposition organisers were determined to muster every possible vote. One lunatic peer was brought in strapped to a chair for his, and possibly other people's, safety. His progress through the voting lobbies could be easily monitored by the sound of his shrieks.

The Duke of Buccleuch and Queensbury, who was once an MP, has recalled hearing an overseas visitor to the House of Commons express alarm at the clanging of the Division Bells, indicating a vote. The tourist had been calmed, however, by a companion who told him: 'Oh, I guess one of them must have escaped.'

Mad Parliament A businesslike and reforming Parliament, summoned in 1258 at Oxford, and maligned by the miffed supporters of Henry III.

It is not to be confused with the Merciless Parliament, summoned in 1388, during Richard II's troubled reign. This was so called because of reprisals taken against members of the Court Party, who had backed the King in his bid to regain the upper hand. But those who applauded such activities called it 'The Parliament that wrought wonders'.

Both episodes left a lasting lesson – that political history depends very much on who is writing it.

Maiden Speech A new MP's ice-breaking performance in the Commons Chamber.

By tradition this effort should avoid controversy, include praise for the Member whom the newcomer has replaced (even if, as is likely, a feud rages betwen them), detail some constituency delights and make passing reference to the topic under debate. By saying nothing, the first-time speaker wins a sympathetic hearing and fulsome congratulations from the next MP called.

Until the maiden speech is under the new MP's belt, he or she cannot ask questions. Most therefore try to get it out of the way as quickly as possible.

Inevitably, some rush things. Take Sir Alan Herbert, who ignored the advice of weathered Commons warriors to delay his initial delivery, and by his own admission 'roared into action' on the second day of the new Parliament. Only to produce what Winston Churchill called 'a brazen hussy of a speech'.

William Cobbett, with equal speed and confidence, began with the words: 'Mr Speaker, it appears to me that since I have been sitting here I have heard a great deal of vain and unprofitable conversation.' And William Cowper, who went on to become Lord Chancellor, addressed the House three times on his first day – winning applause each time.

Lesser mortals are well advised to display more respectful caution as they launch their Commons careers, for even the greats have come a cropper with their earliest utterances in the hallowed Chamber.

Disraeli used his maiden speech to berate Irish MPs and was heckled into silence; Gladstone was reported in the newspapers as having made a few remarks which were inaudible in the Press Gallery.

A more recent rebel was the 22-year-old Mid Ulster by-election winner Bernadette Devlin, who seized her first Parliamentary platform – on the day of her introduction – to deliver a brilliant attack on British policy in Northern Ireland. As she sat down to a few cheers but mostly stunned admiration, Jim Prior turned to Ted Heath and said what a good effort it had been. 'Yes,' replied the Tory leader. 'But it's the only speech she's got in her. She can't make another one.'

Perhaps the judgment proved justified. For Miss Devlin was soon to career across the floor of the House, as words failed her, to box the ears of the then Home Secretary, Reginald Maudling.

Some cruel wits speculated that the notoriously slumberous Mr Maudling had very nearly been woken up by the shocking assault.

Maitland, Lady Olga The daughter of the 17th Earl of Lauderdale has perfect skin . . . and a political hide as tough as a rhino. When not penning gossip columns or leading her pro-Nato pressure group – dubbed by its critics Women, Children, Gymkhanas and Labradors for Defence – she is staking her claim to a Conservative seat.

At the last election Lady Olga put up a spirited campaign in hopeless territory, staging an assault on London's Bethnal Green and Stepney from her base on a luxury yacht moored in St Katherine's Dock. 'I think we've got Brick Lane sewn up,' she was heard to trill, after touring a row of rag trade sweatshops.

The Tory lady had an indomitable canvassing technique. Tripping lightly along an East End thoroughfare, at each of a line of Moslem faces she gushed, 'Congratulations! We're celebrating the end of Ramadan! How marvellous!' Then the blue-blooded candidate slapped a sticker on each handy lapel and continued the jolly banter further down the street.

Until she came to an elderly Cockney, fierce of face and with arms folded angrily.

'What's that we're supposed to be celebrating?' asked the suspicious Eastender.

'We're celebrating a lovely sunny Thursday,' said Lady Olga, swiftly securing yet another sticker before breezing on her way.

This woman could go far.

Major, John First of the Tory intake of 1979 to make the Cabinet, John Major (Huntingdon) was not always so firmly established on the ladder of success. At the age of sixteen he was turned down for a bus conductor's job with London Transport.

The would-be clippy was pitted against an Irishman and a Jamaican woman. With the Irishman swiftly eliminated, the bright youngster then beat the Jamaican in a test of mental arithmetic. She then beat him in a test of physical dexterity – and got the job, as her rival was also thought too tall.

Flunking in physical dexterity must have been especially shaming for John Major, whose father was a conjuror and trapeze artist. Such nimble skills are perfect for politicians, among whom the failed clippy has now recovered his balance.

His patron John Wakeham (Colchester South and Maldon) thinks he possesses 'a safe pair of hands' and, tempting fate, Norman Tebbit has tipped him as a future Prime Minister.

Such is the Thatcherite regard for this man that he is even allowed to get away with admiring Ted Heath. 'He was honest and brave,' ventures Mr Major, though, with an eye to his future career, he adds, 'I did not agree with all he did.'

Mandate A politician who cites a mandate is usually trying to push through an unpopular policy. If it was in the election manifesto, even though few may have spotted it, the proposal is treated as holy writ.

A democratic mandate is supposed to be tied to the winning of majorities. But in Britain the party with an overall majority of seats in the House of Commons never manages a majority of votes in the country. Indeed, the highest popular vote ever amassed by a single grouping was 13,948,883 for Labour in

1951 – the year the Socialists were swept out of office by Winston Churchill's Conservatives. Constituency boundaries, and our first-past-the-post voting system, affect the result considerably.

In British politics the gap between victory and disaster is often tiny. The Tories registered one of their biggest defeats in 1966, when taking 41.9 per cent of the popular vote. In 1987 Mrs Thatcher was returned for a triumphant third term – thanks to 42.3 per cent of those voting. Decimal points can be decisive.

Maps In his days at the Department of Industry, Labour's Tony Benn used to hang a map of Britain on his office wall. Nothing strange in that, of course. Except that the chart was hung upside down.

'It gives you an entirely new perspective,' the left-wing Minister would explain to puzzled visitors.

To help his colleagues keep the correct perspective in their deliberations on world affairs – at a time when much of the globe was still coloured British Empire red – Lord Sankey, Lord Chancellor in the second Labour Government, would take a handy aid to Cabinet meetings. His pocket atlas was often in use.

Marlow, Tony The Conservative MP for Northampton North can outshout even Dennis (Beast of Bolsover) Skinner. Tony Marlow rails against scroungers, immigrants, unions, Europeans and Tory Wets, and heckles his opponents rowdily. He favours a cutting turn of phrase, once attacking an equal pay law as 'an open invitation to any feminist, any harridan, or any rattle-headed female with a chip on her bra-strap to take action against her employer.'

Mason, Roy Ex-Energy Minister Lord (Roy) Mason is near the top of the list of Labour politicians who like to wax lyrical about their deprived childhoods spent foraging for food and sleeping in cardboard boxes.

In his opening speech in the House of Lords, the peer took the process a little further. 'I went underground as a miner at fourteen, and worked for fourteen years in a seam which was one foot ten inches high,' he said. 'Even the mice were bow-legged.'

Mates, Michael Michael Mates (Conservative, East Hampshire), who did *not* lend his name to a newish product of Richard Branson, has been known as 'Rommel' since leading a Tory rebellion on the poll tax. The analogy might appeal to the former Colonel in the Queen's Dragoon Guards.

On the other hand, he will well recall that Rommel lost.

Mellor, David

High-voltage politician (Conservative, Putney) with a short fuse. Master of the crushing put-down, once alleging that SDP-Liberal Alliance by-election winners 'aren't even household names in their own homes.'

Since his outburst of emotion during a trip to the Israeli-occupied West Bank and Gaza, Westminster wags have dubbed him the Unguided Missile.

Members' Smoking Room

MPs – and peers who used to be MPs – mix with the greats in the Members' Smoking Room over tea, coffee or something a little stronger. It is recognised as a neutral zone in the partisan Palace of Westminster, and cross-party friendships flow.

Indeed, so relaxed is the atmosphere that one senior whip once put up a crate of champagne for the MP who could circle the walls of the Smoking Room without touching the ground. Rising to the challenge, a wiry Scottish Member achieved the feat and claimed his prize. He was a keen amateur rock-climber.

It seems, however, that the room has rather declined in popularity since eminent politicians like Winston Churchill, Aneurin Bevan and Harold Macmillan used to hold court there. More MPs now have their own offices where they spend time toiling or relaxing in isolation. Perhaps their workload has also increased.

Or it may be partly to do with the growing dislike of smoking itself, a trend which Mrs Edwina Currie is doing so much to encourage. Lighting up is already banned in the Commons Chamber, division lobbies, Central Lobby and Members' Lobby (until the House has risen), in committee rooms and in part of the library.

The proportion of non-smoking MPs is also rising. For example, among nine Premiers since 1945 five were smokers; but of the five who have held that office since 1963 only Sir Harold Wilson smoked. And, as we now know, even in that case the Prime Ministerial pipe was very rarely lit.

Mistakes

When asked what his greatest mistake had been during his long political career, Enoch Powell replied: 'I've never made a mistake'. Most MPs follow this modest example.

One exception is the bright Labour bruiser Denis Healey. He had a much-publicised row with TV-AM's Anne Diamond

during the last election campaign, after the presenter inquired about the ethics of an operation Mrs Healey had had performed privately.

Most pundits felt the dust-up had been unwise, and in a subsequent interview Mr Healey seemed to agree. He said, 'I made a great mistake of trying to hit her adviser . . . instead of her'.

MPs

'Your representative owes you, not his industry only, but his judgement; and he betrays, instead of serving you, if he sacrifices it to your opinion,' said the political philosopher Edmund Burke in a classic 1774 address to the electors of Bristol. And such a principle may still ring true.

If, however, an MP is rash enough to disregard the views of his or her voters too often, come the next election the verdict in the ballot boxes is likely to be one of sweet revenge.

Naming

An over-excited MP who refuses to shut up, sit down or retract a slur, risks being named for contempt of the Speaker. The rebel is expelled from the Commons for the day. Force may be used if necessary.

Once it seemed that the gracious Tory backbencher Dame Irene Ward would have to be dragged out, when she occupied the (Labour) Government front bench and refused to budge. The Serjeant at Arms was summoned, offered Dame Irene his arm and she accepted it. The courtly couple swept out as if for an evening stroll.

An apology (as offered by Michael Heseltine after his attempt at some drum majorette practice with the Mace) makes good any insult. But a refusal to say sorry can result in suspension (on full pay) from the House.

A vote normally kicks out a first-time villain for five working days. But a second offence in one Parliamentary session involves a 20-day suspension. A third outbreak of hooliganism could see the culprit sent packing for an indefinite period – until MPs feel the lesson has been learned.

Such a sharply rising scale of punishment may explain why, while some MPs are prepared to break the rules once, recurrent gross offenders are rare.

National Front

The far-right faction has now splintered. But in its mid-1970s heyday it threatened a political breakthrough by building a coalition of skinheads, football hooligans, racists, neo-Nazis and nice old ladies who thought they were voting for the political wing of the National Trust.

Nineteen Twenty Two Committee

The grouping of all Conservative MPs, which was founded in a take-no-prisoners plot of October 1922.

At that time, unhappy Tory Members met in the Carlton Club and engineered both the ending of the Coalition Government and the downfall of Austen Chamberlain as Conservative leader in the House of Commons.

Soon the 1922 body was embracing every Conservative backbencher, and down the years has come to meet regularly to discuss pending business. But Tory leaders have guarded against further nights of the long knives, and those who have not have done so at their peril. Hello, Edward Heath.

The head of the 1922 Committee is a senior and long-serving MP who briefs the party leader on backbench opinion. Mrs Thatcher has been particularly careful to protect her back, and meetings are frequent.

The 1922 Committee is somewhat similar to the Parliamentary Labour Party, but in public the former likes to show more united loyalty to the leadership than does the latter. In private, gloves can come off.

Both groupings meet in larger committee rooms of the Commons. Inevitably more intimate, Social and Liberal Democratic meetings can be held in the cafeteria. And the Owenite SDP can easily sort things out in a lift, taxi, or telephone kiosk.

Noble Perks Peers possess the anachronistic right of an individual audience with the Sovereign. Exercising such a noble perk has, however, been discouraged ever since Queen Victoria announced that she found it 'extremely inconvenient'.

Certain lords have also claimed an ancient right to remain hatted in the presence of the monarch. One, a previous Lord Kingsale, boasted of such a privilege by marching up and down in front of Queen Victoria with his hat firmly over his eyes.

The unamused Victoria tolerated the display for some moments before her patience snapped. 'Kingsale,' she finally said in a voice that could not be ignored. 'Don't be silly. Take it off.'

Official Monster Raving Loony Party The barmy brainchild of singer David 'Screaming Lord' Sutch, who first stood for Parliament against Harold Wilson, at Huyton, in 1964. In those days he campaigned on the Teenage Party ticket, favouring such things as the lowering of the voting age to eighteen and the legalising of commercial radio. Sheer madness, of course.

Raving proposals at the last General Election included:

- Converting EEC butter mountains into ski slopes;
- Stocking wine lakes with mackerel and herring which, when harvested, would be ready soused. Just add onions for delicious hors d'oeuvres;
- Privatising hot air from the House of Commons. (Loonies insisted that there would be enough warm air to heat half the nation's homes.)

Party chairman Alan Hope is already a town councillor in Devon, winning his place because the seat was uncontested. 'It was all a mistake,' he wails.

Sadly, with stiffer competition for Westminster, any loonies in the present Parliament are entirely unofficial.

Official Secrets Act The workings of Whitehall are covered by a blanket Official Secrets Act, under which it is illegal for tea ladies to reveal the colour of a Minister's wallpaper or favourite brand of biscuit.

Richard Shepherd (Conservative, Aldridge-Brownhills), who led the latest attempt at reform, points out that if secret service house-breakers go to the wrong address and raid your home by mistake, by reporting the matter to the police you can be arrested for breaking the Official Secrets Act. So tread carefully. (*See* **Secrets**)

Oldest Member

The oldest Member of Parliament ever was Lord 'Manny' Shinwell (1884–1986). He first sat in the House of Commons in November 1922, and was still attending the House of Lords until shortly before his death aged 101 years and 202 days.

Towards the end, the once-fiery Socialist was making speeches that even his best friends found impossible to fathom. But all agreed that Lord Shinwell was a splendid survivor. The point was vividly illustrated when a chunk of ceiling masonry crashed on to the bench normally occupied by the almost-centenarian peer. Luckily, he was absent from his seat at the time.

Opportunism

'I would rather be an opportunist and float than go to the bottom with my principles round my neck,' said Tory Prime Minister Stanley Baldwin, stating bluntly a secret motto shared by many successful politicians.

John Wilkes, a radical politician of the late 18th century, was equally keen to maximise his support – by trimming his sails or seeking unlikely allies if need be. At one hustings meeting in Middlesex, a heckler bellowed, 'I would rather vote for the devil than for John Wilkes.'

To which the pushy politician replied, 'And if your friend is not standing?'

At times, opportunism may take precedence over grief for ambitious politicians. Throwing caution and good taste to the wind, an eager prospective candidate once telephoned the national agent within hours of an MP's death. 'I am so sorry to hear that Mr X has died,' he said. 'Is there any chance of me taking his place?'

'Yes,' answered the national agent curtly. 'If the undertaker has no objection.'

Opposition

The Whig Premier Lord Melbourne and his arch Tory rival, the Duke of Wellington, shared one basic belief: both thought that all new legislation, however desirable, was to be deplored.

Sir Frederick Banbury went even further. He opposed every Bill that was brought before Parliament while he was a Member.

Outside Employment

Many MPs, especially on the Conservative benches, do not give up their former employment once elected. They could argue that this is a safety net against future defeat, or that knowledge of the outside commercial world aids their work at Westminster.

Whatever the excuse, most electors affected will not realise that they are represented by a part-timer (this fact is never a feature of the manifesto).

Some say, unfairly, that the Parliamentary day is arranged so that lawyer MPs can appear in court in the morning and afternoon, to arrive at the Commons at tea-time.

Other Members flit frequently between Parliament and their company directorships or City desks. And retained farms in the distant shires, though probably run by managers or relatives, will need regular inspection.

Labour MPs – drawn from the ranks of teachers and lecturers, local government workers and trade union officials – do not usually have the advantage of outside salaries or private incomes. But are they any more effective for their longer hours of political toil?

The Labour benches in the Commons Chamber are certainly deserted at least as often as those on the Tory side.

Owen, David A politician who made a name for himself as a dashing Health Minister and a glamorous Foreign Secretary, and who made a potential mint by doing up two derelict Thames-side houses in London's then-unfashionable Docklands.

His complex character combines great judgement and great vanity. His friends and foes are divided on which quality comes most often to the fore. The same people disagree on whether Dr Death (SDP, Plymouth Devonport) is the new Messiah or the new Mosley of British politics. Time will tell.

Since leaving the Labour Party, and later splitting with the Liberals and with most Social Democrats, David Owen has appeared something of a captain without a crew. But there is no truth in the rumour that he has been offered the lead role in the TV series *Ever Decreasing Circles*.

Still a medic at heart, Dr Owen clearly wishes that politics were more like the GP's surgery. People with problems come for advice and prescriptions which should soothe or cure them. Precious few care or dare to argue.

Financially at least, he could give up the quest for high office tomorrow and simply contemplate his naval dockyard constituency. Besides a wealth of real estate, his wife Debbie makes a fortune as a literary agent. She modestly claims that success in this field couldn't be simpler: just find two authors, and you're away. She began with Jeffrey Archer and Barbara Cartland.

Pairing A discreet Commons liaison of which MPs' wives (and a few husbands) are the greatest supporters, as it may help them see their spouses just a little more often.

Pairing arrangements are where one MP agrees to 'pair off' with another from the Opposition, so that they can both miss all but essential late-night votes and get home early . . . or appear in their local before closing time.

As demand exceeds supply, there is a frantic rush by Government supporters to welcome new Opposition Members and woo them into partnership. But the new boys and girls are well advised to be choosy when selecting a mate.

An elderly Government backer, an MP for a marginal seat or a Member whose majority could vanish in pending boundary-changes are not good bets for a long-term relationship. The ideal candidates are youngish, with safe seats and brilliant brains – preferably fair set for ministerial posts that will mean demanding duties outside Parliament.

With such happy link-ups, new MPs' marriages may stay intact and their ulcers dormant.

Palace of Westminster

Don't be fooled by the title. The accommodation in Sir Charles Barry's Gothic revivalist pile is nothing like palatial. The stately exterior conceals a warren of often airless and windowless passages, cul-de-sacs, cubby-holes and black holes of Calcutta.

Within these cramped confines 2,000 employees toil in conditions that would not be tolerated by even the most Dickensian of factory inspectors. Which could be one of the reasons why the House (along with other Royal palaces) is exempted from such scrutiny, while additional work space is slowly being increased in the vicinity of Parliament Square.

A few months after the exhilaration of electoral victory, many first-time MPs have abandoned naive hopes of high office. All their energies are expended on learning the layout of a building that makes Hampton Court Maze look open-plan.

By now they should at least know their way around the newest bit of the building – the debating Chamber itself. Barry's original was demolished by bombs in 1941. The present Chamber, opened in 1950, was designed by Sir Giles Gilbert Scott. Despite minor scuffs and scuffles, it has so far suffered less from private and official vandalism than have the great man's beautiful red telephone boxes.

But how to connect the 1,200-strong mass of committee rooms, bars and restaurants, chess and TV dens, offices, gift kiosk, library, loos, baths and barber's shop that are crammed haphazardly into every Westminster nook and cranny?

Unfortunately the two miles of Parliamentary passages do not benefit from a yellow line of the type that pedestrians seeking out the Barbican find so indispensable. A useful colour guide is provided by the benches, however. Green means the bemused Member must still be in the Commons; red says that a wrong turning has been taken into the House of Lords.

It's all enough to cause depression, despondency or even despair. However, most youthful backbenchers – especially those whose Parliamentary base has not yet extended beyond a cupboard – soon take heart again. They come to realise that

P Parliamentary Private Secretaries

pressing for promotion into the more spacious corridors of power is the only chance they'll get of finding their feet . . . and stretching their legs.

Parliamentary Private Secretaries PPS means a last-minute thought – and as in letters so, frequently, in politics.

The Parliamentary Private Secretary is the lowest form of governmental life, called forth from a list of backbenchers kept by the Chief Whip and approved by the Prime Minister.

A PPS-ship may be a reward for devoted service made to those unsuited for ministerial office, or a method of buying off MPs made troublesome by thwarted ambition. Or it can be a starting point for genuine high-fliers. An MP should realise into which category he or she falls, before accepting the promotion call with delight or dogged duty.

Some will find it an unrewarding straitjacket. They may no longer ask questions or make speeches on subjects covered by their particular Minister. Instead, their boss must be kept supplied with favourable questions, with a 'pair' when called away from the Commons, and with latest news of party opinion.

Sitting in on departmental briefings, a clever PPS – though barred from seeing secret papers – may become involved in policy issues. Others, squeezed between a political adviser and the Minister's Principal Private Secretary (a career civil servant), remain dogsbodies. If after two years no promotion is yet in sight, the wise MP will return to backbench freedom.

But real power is held by the Prime Minister's PPS. Such an MP briefs the Chief Whip before an impending reshuffle and is the Premier's trusty link to the party. The mere arrival of this somewhat sinister figure at backbench meetings can be enough to silence criticism. Not for nothing was Mrs Thatcher's former PPS Ian Gow (Conservative, Eastbourne) dubbed 'Supergrass' by his alleged victims.

This is not a post for anyone fearful of making lasting enemies. But promise of ministerial office or minor honour hardens many hearts.

Parties (I) What politicians group themselves into, to seek power. The necessity of such linkages makes for some strange and unsuited bedfellows. Which can in turn make for tensions, feuds and vendettas.

Indeed, some politicians spend entire careers convinced that their real enemies sit on their side.

Harold Wilson was an expert in such matters. He once observed that whenever the then Prime Minister, Harold Macmillan, returned from a trip abroad, Rab Butler would go to the airport and grab him warmly by the throat.

Parties (II) The non-political variety are also attractive to certain men and women of power – and the constant round of balls, receptions and premières in the capital features many Westminster faces.

Most socialising remains private. The Tory MP seen dancing on a tabletop cheek to cheek with a glamorous millionairess had long given up hope of ministerial office. Even so, publicity would have been unwanted.

Prolific party-goer David Steel won the sympathy of friend and foe alike when, as cameras clicked, a TV actress perfected a clever publicity push and knocked him to the floor in a festive fall.

Mr Steel, who had survived the far worse embarrassment of recording a disco tune entitled *I Feel Liberal*, managed to retain a little dignity and a slightly frozen smile. His colleagues rallied in support.

'I don't know what all the fuss is about,' said one, with tongue in cheek. 'Gladstone was always helping fallen women.'

Party Political Broadcasts Helpful, objective information slots by the major political groupings. Or, to put it another way, boring propaganda breaks during which you make a cup of tea.

Pay During the Profumo scandal – which featured a Cabinet Minister, call girls and a Soviet officer – Harold Wilson commented on relative values.

'Saturday's papers told of an opportunist nightclub proprietor who had offered Miss Christine Keeler – or should I refer to her as Christine Keeler Ltd? – a nightclub job at a salary of £5,000 a week. I say to the Prime Minister that there is something utterly nauseating about a system of society which pays a harlot 25 times as much as its Prime Minister, 250 times as much as it pays its Members of Parliament and 500 times as much as it pays some of its ministers of religion.'

Today's politicians, in real and in relative terms, are rewarded rather more generously. But whether society is any less nauseating because of it must be a moot point.

Parliamentarians have always moaned about their finances. At the time of the 1832 Reform Act, when children cleaned chimneys for pennies, Lord Durham maintained that a man could 'jog along' on £40,000 a year. And Lord Clive, with large estates to care for, was already feeling the pinch. 'I am amazed at my moderation,' he declared.

In 1985, Lord Gowrie declared himself to be unable to manage on a ministerial wage of around £30,000 a year. Had he waited he would have seen political salaries receive hefty rises and long-sought linkage with senior civil servants. Even so, the £34,688 the peer would have been paid in 1988 was peanuts in comparison with his returns as chairman of Sotheby's.

One curiosity is that the salary list from the Treasury includes the Leader of the Opposition (£48,148 in 1988), three whips and his leader in the Lords. Even so, whatever party they come from, they take every opportunity to bite the hand that feeds them. (*See* **Expenses**)

Peers

Members of the House of Lords began as leaders of brigand bands. They were summoned to Parliament so that the King could keep an eye on them and lean on them for loot. Later they tended to be leisurely aristocrats, who travelled up to town occasionally from rural retreats, and who regarded Westminster as a congenial club. These days they are a very mixed bunch indeed.

First there are historical relics (*see* **Lords Spiritual**). The Duke of Norfolk is among such splendid survivals. Though he takes the title Chief Butler of England, at his stately seat of Arundel Castle he has others do the leg-work for him. Fellow hereditary peers are now engaged in commoner pursuits. The third Lord Calverley is better known as PC Muff of the West Yorkshire Constabulary; and Lord Nelson has recently retired from the Hertfordshire force. Eton-educated Lord Teviot is a former Brighton bus driver.

Since 1958 the Upper House has been boosted by an influx of sundry life peers. A major donation to the Conservative Party may ensure elevation, though all parties profess shock that Lloyd George employed touts brazenly to sell seats. Less-flush Labour hopefuls must settle for years of trade union toil and ennoblement when they are nearing their dotage. Only 15 per cent of peers do not qualify for a bus pass.

Despite getting pretty rebellious over the Rabbits Bill of 1928, their lordships were always thought a solidly Tory lot. They had confirmed this impression in a note to the Conservative Premier Arthur Balfour.

'We agree with whatever you want to do,' it read. 'Whatever it may be.'

Nowadays they are far less partisan. And indeed, governments may have good cause to regard them as revolting for peers can act as a check on power-grabbing parties of any persuasion.

The Upper House offers its members up to £100 a day to take part in a civilised debating society and a legislative chamber which gets to grips with details the Commons hasn't had time for. Reports of its death have been proved exaggerated.

Personal Experience

It is sometimes said that MPs are keenest to effect reforms when they have personal experience of the wrong to be righted.

Certainly when the Gordon rioters of 1780 smashed the windows of the Palace of Westminster, the urgency of the hour was suddenly impressed on Parliamentary opinion most vividly. And the Victorian clamour for decent sewers was joined by MPs when the stench from a filthy Thames could no longer be ignored in Commons corridors.

Petitions

Although rarely persuading MPs to change their minds on any issue, the petition to Parliament has been a popular method of mobilising public opinion since Saxon times. Indeed, Parliament may have begun in meetings of the King's Council, called to consider such submissions.

A Commons committee report of 1640 records:

> "This Committee was appointed to peruse a Petition, that was enclosed in the Cover of a Letter, addressed to the Parliament, and found upon Salisbury Plain; and, being brought to the Mayor of Salisbury, was by him sent up to Serjeant Hide, a Member of this House, and by him this Day offered to the House.
>
> The Committee, after they had perused it, found it of no better Consequence than to be burnt."

Before 1974, signatures on petitions were counted by staff in Parliament's Journal Office. They were, at one time, paid 2s 6d per thousand names, and might have amassed a fortune in former times. The Great Chartist petition of 1848 numbered more than 5.7 million names. After checking, however, only 1,975,496 were accepted. Discounted signatures included Victoria Rex, Mr Punch and someone called No Cheese. Strict scrutiny ensued.

Petitions must be worded in 'respectful, decorous and temperate' terms and may be sent free in the post. They can be presented verbally by an MP with a publicity-seeking flourish, or slipped quietly into a large green bag hooked on the back of the Speaker's Chair.

Each petition is then passed to the relevant Minister, who will usually see that a written reply to the case is laid before the House. Action rarely follows.

Phibbs, Harry

An unfortunate name for any young, would-be upwardly-mobile politician.

This radical right-winger further failed to gain the confidence of his Conservative elders when he accused Lord Stockton, shortly before the statesman's death, of having been a war criminal. And his antics with the Federation of Conservative Students caused Nanny, in the form of the then party chairman Norman Tebbit, to put her foot down hard.

A copy-book well and truly blotted.

Plaid Cymru

The Welsh Nationalist Party, with three MPs, which puts the heat on imperialist England over its policies for the Principality. Some Members have been prepared to starve themselves to death for a TV channel which sub-titles soap operas in Welsh.

But Plaid Cymru condemns extreme Celts who bring even more heat into the argument by setting fire to English-owned second homes.

Plots

Clever politicians are generally cunning plotters, choosing the best opportunity to further their cause – and being well-versed in the art of the calculated risk. But if a plot backfires, the result can be disaster for the conspirators. Politics is short of second chances.

As Harold Wilson, who stalked Downing Street in fear of Cabinet conspiracies, once warned, 'In the game of musical daggers, never be left holding the dagger when the music stops.'

Politicians & Politics

> "A politician is a statesman who approaches every question with an open mouth.
> (Adlai Stevenson)
>
> He knows nothing and thinks he knows everything . . .
>
> That points to a political career.
> (from George Bernard Shaw's play *Major Barbara*).
>
> A politician is a man who divides his time between running for office and running for cover. (Anon.)
>
> A politician is a man who stands for what he believes others will fall for. (Anon.)
>
> Politics is the art of looking for trouble, finding it whether it exists or not, diagnosing it incorrectly and applying the wrong remedy."
> (Sir Ernest Benn)

Postage

Members of Parliament are entitled to free first class post anywhere in the United Kingdom, provided they are writing on Parliamentary or constituency business. Letters to loved ones, creditors or Father Christmas do not count.

From 1660, MPs were given the privilege of sending letters free by signing their names on the cover. Some kindly Members took to signing packets of covers for their friends. Until, by 1837, nearly seven-and-a-half million of these autographed missives were mailed in a single year – costing the postal service over £1 million in lost revenue.

Certain free-loading MPs did not limit their franking privilege to letters. Furniture and even a pack of hounds were held to be covered by it; and one Irish Member franked his wife and family for a holiday from Galway to Dublin and back. Such behaviour helped get the privilege abolished when the penny post was introduced in 1840.

There was also a time when the public could send a letter to their MP free of charge, so long as they stated clearly on the envelope that they had penned lines of official business. Now a stampless missive means that a Member has to pay the excess rate – unless it is addressed to a Minister, in which case postal sorters tend to turn a blind eye to the absence of the sticky-backed Queen's head.

If sitting for a marginal constituency, an MP will probably cough up the cash due on each unstamped envelope. If his seat is safe, he may plead poverty . . . and give silent thanks for a slightly smaller postbag.

Postbag

Answering letters from constituents is an unavoidable chore for MPs who wish to be re-elected.

Those who sit for safe seats may have cards printed in a few stock formats, advising constituents that their complaints have been passed to other agencies; but most will take great pains to get at least the PR right.

Rare indeed is the MP who answers a query with the following brevity: 'Dear Mr Smith. No. Yours sincerely . . .' It has happened, however. Normally even a complete rebuff is couched in polite thanks for receipt of 'interesting' views.

All MPs are at times plagued by obsessive writers who will not let go of an obscure point. Most put a brave face on it. One, driven to distraction after a deluge of manic missives from a mad constituent, wrote on the following lines:

> Dear Sir, I fear you are being impersonated. A complete lunatic is using your name and address and writing the most absurd rubbish to me. Perhaps you would like to make inquiries? Yours faithfully . . .

He wasn't troubled again.

Posters

An essential part of any election campaign is the poster, and parties go to great lengths to get the message right. Faked dole queues have been particularly popular on hoardings in recent years . . .

At the last election, Labour's advertising agency paid volunteers £25 each to pose as job-seekers outside a bogus unemployment exchange in East London. The result was an eye-catching political poster deploring the length of Britain's dole queues.

Tory cries of foul play were rather muted. For in 1979 they had hired Young Conservatives to look redundant beneath the powerful slogan 'Labour Isn't Working'.

Posters **P**

As each Election Campaign advances and the poster war hots up, trees are often pressured to declare their intention of voting Conservative, while derelict houses are coaxed into siding with Labour.

One attractive council candidate in Liverpool recently produced fetching posters which were snapped up like hot cakes and placed in many windows. A second printing was equally popular – though, sadly, over-inking had given the lady a distinctive moustache. And in a third, still-inkier, edition she began to resemble George V.

The council contender, a Liberal, scored a thumping victory. But some voters must have concluded that she was well advanced on a drastic course of male hormone injections.

Powell, Enoch A man of burning eyes and conviction, Tory-turned-Ulster Unionist Enoch Powell can take two perfectly logical propositions and mix them in surprising ways. He fell out with the Conservative leadership in 1969, with a speech which included the line: 'Like the Roman I seem to see "the river Tiber foaming with much blood".'

Rather than predicting an imminent disaster in Italy, he was warning against coloured immigration into Britain. Mr Powell has returned regularly to the theme ever since.

Having lost his South Down seat at the last election, and long fumed against the folly of life peerages, Enoch Powell is now out in the political cold.

Meanwhile, he has seen his usual place at the State Opening of Parliament taken by Diane Abbott (Labour, Hackney North and Stoke Newington), Britain's first black woman MP.

Power Power is what politics is about, but where can you find it? In Parliament ultimately, though bullied MPs must feel that at Westminster the whips rule. Meanwhile whips themselves hope to be *en route* to higher reaches of Government.

A new MP will need to be noticed as a politician of depth and dependability. Prolonged periods of silence, punctuated by sage noddings of the head, are thus advisable. Then, if the parent party is in office, painfully slow promotion may follow – from Parliamentary Private Secretary to Under Secretary to Minister of State to full Minister.

After such exhausting progress, the now-ageing politician may enter the Cabinet. But even there power is unevenly spread, as a spending Minister finds when pressing the departmental demand for funds each year.

If resisting gentle pressure to cut a claim, a spendthrift Minister is hauled before the Star Chamber – a committee comprising the Chancellor, Chief Financial Secretary to the Treasury and other senior Ministers – who conduct a trial in the manner of the historic court after which it is named. The brazen spender is mercilessly broken.

Increasingly, power is said to rest in one pair of hands (those belonging to the Prime Minister) though occupants of Downing Street themselves perceive threats from civil servants, apparent political allies, diehard enemies and, of course, the wicked media.

And by the time a Premier feels truly in control, an election is sure to be due. As the leader's belongings are packed for a speedy exit from Downing Street, in case the verdict of the voters for some absurd reason proves negative, the most powerful person in the land suddenly looks very humble indeed.

Prison

Politicians from John Wilkes to John Stonehouse have found themselves transferred from the dungeons of Westminster to proper prisons. But down the centuries a jail term has been more an occupational hazard for journalists, seeking to report on the ways of public figures.

The charge of libel has loomed large. Former editor of the satirical magazine *Private Eye*, Richard Ingrams, once failed to obey an injunction during a court action taken by the financier Sir James Goldsmith. Staring the strong risk of incarceration firmly in the face, he confessed: 'The only thing I really worry about in going to prison is the thought of Lord Longford coming to visit me.'

Privilege

MPs are liable to arrest on a criminal charge. They cannot, however, be prosecuted for sedition or sued for libel or slander in respect of anything said during proceedings of Parliament or published in its Order Paper.

The aim is to protect Members while they carry out their duty to raise vital questions in the House, questions which might otherwise be silenced by the threat of action for defamation.

Critics add that it has also allowed certain MPs to make wild and unsubstantiated charges without fear of having to prove their words in court.

Purges

'The first essential for a Prime Minister is to be a good butcher,' said William Ewart Gladstone, and those who have followed him have tried to heed the Grand Old Man's words.

Urbane Harold Macmillan was notoriously nimble with the carving knife of dismissal when wishing to slice out offending Cabinet Ministers. After driving the dagger home he would enjoy a hearty dinner and a gentle novel by his beloved Anthony Trollope.

Harold Wilson used to snap that dogs that barked and bit would not get their licences renewed. And Margaret Thatcher, while professing distaste for showing a chap the door, has turned Downing Street into a veritable slaughterhouse of Tory Wets. Gladstone would have been impressed.

Q Question Time

Question Time

Question Time lasts for about an hour on Mondays to Thursdays while the House is sitting. At 3.15 pm on Tuesdays and Thursdays the star bat, the Prime Minister, walks to the wicket.

Providing much of the drama of the political week, Question Time gives MPs who have been dutifully slogging away on some complex and perhaps crashingly dull committee a chance to let off steam and enjoy a spectacle.

But the Government batsmen and women are far more likely to hit sixes than to be caught in the slips. For they have come prepared – an MP wishing to ask an oral question must lodge it with the Table Office two weeks in advance.

The fun of Question Time is not in the original query but the supplementary question that a Member is allowed to ask once the Minister has dealt with the opening shot. There are usually about 60 questions tabled each day, but only the first 20 are likely to be dealt with in the time available. Government supporters are only too keen to help Ministers by bowling easy balls planned in advance.

A fortnight before the Minister's monthly innings at the Question Time crease, the luminary's Parliamentary Private Secretary will collar a loyal backbencher to table a question already prepared. Providing that the query then comes within the first 20 in the ensuing ballot, the helpful MP will find a supplementary waiting for him on the letter board when Question Time looms.

Questions to the Prime Minister form the Commons' most popular spectator sport. The participants may or may not enjoy the proceedings. Harold Macmillan felt physically sick before entering the Chamber each Tuesday and Thursday; Harold Wilson relished the prospect of a grand performance and Mrs Thatcher has admitted to a touch of stage fright.

The Iron Lady once confessed to Radio Four's *Woman's Hour* of the struggle to compose herself. 'I think – now look love, keep calm, concentrate,' she said. But few viewers and listeners will detect so much as a quake or a quiver as the Prime Minister hits sixes into every corner of the Chamber.

And don't imagine that there is much spontaneity at Question Time. Most MPs will have prepared their every phrase for maximum impact. Those who don't weigh every word can easily come unstuck, as did Dame Irene Ward during a famous exchange:

> **Dame Irene:** When are the Wrens going to get their uniforms?
>
> **Minister:** Sailors first.
>
> **Dame Irene:** Is my Right Honourable Friend saying that Wrens' skirts must be held up until all sailors have been satisfied?

Queues Queues of hopeful visitors to the House of Commons begin forming during matinée Question Time performances, and are often still snaking back towards Westminster Tube station in the early evening.

It is virtually impossible for a casual visitor to gain immediate entry during questions from 2.30 to 3.30 pm, or during an important debate. Admission orders for 140 of the 157 seats in the Strangers' Gallery are issued in advance to Members, each of whom receives two every third week on an alphabetical rota system. Having entertained constituents to a cup of tea and a tour of the Westminster works, they are glad to be able to get shot of them into the Gallery.

As the evening wears on, however, ticket-holders tend to drift away – especially if the business of the House is taken up with tedious detail. So those who have been waiting patiently outside have a chance of late reward. Sadly for them, however, they are likely to find that, by the time they enter, the Chamber is largely deserted.

If thwarted after a long wait for the Commons Chamber, one can always try the House of Lords. Though spectator space is limited, there is less demand. And even if the debate is dull, the surroundings are splendid.

Quorum A quorum of the Commons is 40, including the Speaker – and before 1971 a Member could call a count to check that the minimum number of MPs was present. If fewer than 40 could get to the Chamber within two minutes, the House was 'counted out' and adjourned for the day.

Now time is deemed too tight to waste. So if fewer than 40 Members (including tellers and the Chair) take part in a division, the business being considered is held over until the next sitting, and the House goes on to deal with subsequent orders of the day. The green benches can thus be left safely empty during many debates.

In the House of Lords – with more members than the Commons but with stiff competition from grouse moors, clubs and private beaches – a quorum is just three. If, however, fewer than 30 peers have voted on a question relating to a Bill or to delegated legislation (a statutory order arising out of an Act), the Lord Chancellor or Chairman declares that no decision has been reached. The debate on that particular item stands adjourned.

Racist Accused of being a racist by a fellow member of a radio discussion panel, Rochdale MP Cyril Smith retorted: 'Me a racist? Never. I'll have you know that only the other day I had twelve Asians for lunch at the House of Commons.'

Cue for studio audience to erupt into uncontrolled laughter.

Randy A trait of all MPs and political activists, which finds physical expression at least once every five years.

The origins of the word are obscure. But Henry Fielding's *Don Quixote* carried the immortal line, 'He was randying for a knight of his acquaintance with no less than 600 freeholders at his heels.'

'To randy' means 'to canvas for support', of course.

Records Parliament would by now be knee-deep in paper, were its records not neatly stored away on five-and-a-half miles of steel shelving. The Clerk of the Records of the House is in charge of some 3,000,000 documents – including every Act that has been passed since 1497, papers laid on the Table of the Lords since 1531, and most Commons records surviving from 1547.

Printed copies of Acts of Parliament go on sale to the public through Her Majesty's Stationery Office as soon as possible after Royal Assent. In addition, two master copies of each law are specially printed. One is sent to the Public Record Office, the Government's record store outside Parliament. The other is added to the vast archives in Victoria Tower, at the opposite end of the Palace of Westminster to Big Ben (serious students welcome, on written application).

Records come in all shapes and sizes. Some of the historical parchments are particularly cumbersome. One Act dealing with taxation, passed during the reign of George III, extends to 440 yards in length. Now shelves of tapes have also been added, which please the purists with a record of every Parliamentary cough and sneeze.

The Victoria Tower's twelve air-conditioned floors still have space for documents from many decades to come. Purpose-built by Barry as a fireproof store for Parliamentary and legal records, the Tower and its contents are as safe from the hazards and ravages of time as modern scientific precautions can make them.

Should nuclear war be signalled, senior politicians may join the rest of us in the frying pan, but the contents of the Records Office will have been trundled to safety in an underground bunker at Corsham, Wiltshire.

And there Martian archaeologists of the 25th century will discover them, and make of them what they may.

The Red Flag A banner that has fluttered over certain Socialist-run city halls, and a leftist anthem sung at the end of Labour conferences – though TV cameras relate that the words are still a mystery to many delegates.

There is an alternative tongue-in-cheek version, which dispenses with the raising of the scarlet standard high, and the jeering at cowards who flinch and traitors who sneer. It has been a favourite of Liberal gatherings, and runs like this:

> The People's Flag is slightly pink
> It's not as red as some folks think.
> We must not let the people know
> What Socialists thought long ago.
>
> Don't let the scarlet banner float
> We need the middle classes' vote.
> Though our old-fashioned comrades
> sneer
> We'll stay in power for many a year.

Red Tape Wound tightly around the workings of Westminster and Whitehall, this provides ideal insulation against the chill winds of public scrutiny. Local councils and the European Parliament favour double layers for extra protection.

A little length of red tape is also standard issue for new MPs, so that they can hang up their swords in the cloakrooms (along with their cloaks). Indeed, such a ribbon and a locker key are the only guaranteed items in the just-elected Member's Welcome to Westminster pack.

Whether the new boys and girls receive such trivial things as desks and telephones is in the lap of the gods. That is, the whips (*see* **Whipping**). And to offend these all-powerful party policemen means to go without.

Revenge Those who live by the sword shall die by it so they say, and the field of politics is littered with the corpses of sabre-tongued talents who have jabbed at their enemies, only to be impaled in return. Insults can sometimes boomerang on the accusing party.

Perhaps the sweetest and subtlest form of revenge is therefore to confound your critics by achieving great success. For a politician, Clement Attlee was a man of retiring disposition and few words. ('I saw an empty taxi arrive and Clement Attlee got out,' ran one snide aside.) Leading the Labour Party to unexpected electoral victory in 1945, however, the little man had the last laugh.

In later life he composed a verse in which he stylishly thumbed his nose at his critics. It ran like this:

> Few thought he was even a starter.
> There were many who thought themselves smarter.
> But he ended PM,
> CH and OM,
> An Earl and a Knight
> Of the Garter.

Rifles Since the rise of mainland terrorism, security could scarcely be stricter at Westminster. There are over 100 police officers on duty when the House is sitting, and visitors must pass through stringent screening.

Yet while every effort is taken to ensure that firearms are not smuggled into the building, guns are on hire in the basement beneath the House of Lords. Political sharpshooters are able to unwind by setting their sights on rifle range bull's eyes.

When not targeting high office, Junior Minister Mrs Edwina Currie is an active rifle club member. Ever ready to share her thoughts with a passing Pressman, she admits, 'I do occasionally think of my political opponents when I take aim.'

Richard the Lion Heart A statue of Richard Coeur de Lion, the crusading British king who spent more time on foreign trips than even the cleverest MP has managed, stands outside the Houses of Parliament in Old Palace Yard.

With sword raised aloft, the statue has been seen as an emblem of national determination . . . especially when the weapon was bent by a bomb, in 1940. A great debate ensued as to whether the sword should remain crumpled as a symbol of endurance – like the nation, it might bend but would not break.

However, with fears that visitors would merely regard the mauled metal as a sign of shoddy workmanship rather than heroic resistance, the sword was straightened.

Rosettes These come in various colours and tend to be pinned to political candidates and prize show animals.

Rotten Boroughs A term that might now be used to describe blighted inner-city areas, it in fact dates back to the days before the passing of the

1832 Great Reform Bill. Rotten Boroughs were constituencies that were open to offers. Of cash, that is.

Bribery and corruption flourished at elections during the 18th and early 19th centuries, and there was a brisk trade in Parliamentary seats. Some were even publicly advertised for sale.

Besides wealthy patrons, purchasers of rotten (or pocket) boroughs also included candidates who wished to sit as independents and who were rich enough to pursue their pleasure. Most representatives, however, were merely the nominees of powerful local interests who paid the piper and expected to call the tune.

At a time when the 133,000 citizens of Manchester were entirely unrepresented in the Commons, one of the rottenest boroughs, Old Sarum, in Wiltshire, could not even provide shelter for the Returning Officer. Here, however, seven voters sent two MPs to Parliament.

Then there was the Suffolk port of Dunwich. Long after most of the town had slipped into the sea, its fourteen electors continued to return a brace of Members.

Worst of all was the case of the Cornish fishing village of Bossiney, whose single voter after 1782 had sole say in choosing an MP.

At the opposite end of the scale, the 217,900 voters of Hendon in 1941 – Britain's largest-ever constituency electorate – thought they had a rotten chance of making their vote count. So the seat was cut up by the Boundary Commission.

Royalty

Edmund Burke believed that kingship depended on putting on a good show. 'Strip majesty of its exteriors (its first and last letters) and its becomes "a jest",' he said.

The State Opening of Parliament shows monarchy at its most majestic, with the Queen suffering silently under the weight of her heavy crown. She will have had no say in the speech she recites, outlining the Government's planned programme. But HM long ago made clear that she wanted a script that was both short and readable.

When the ceremony is over the monarch is waved off in the State Coach by cheering crowds. MPs, meanwhile, are being read the Outlawries Bill – a tradition which dates from 1603 and underlines that they are not compelled to give priority to the Sovereign's business. Antiquity has softened the rudeness of the gesture.

On one evening each week the Prime Minister is driven to Buckingham Palace for a Royal audience. The talk is secret, but the Premier will bring news of major issues of the day. The Queen, who has seen countless Cabinets come and go, may advise by anecdote about a similar incident in the past.

As a constitutional monarch the Queen has little real power – except, perhaps, in the event of a hung or balanced parliament when she might have to adjudicate between rival claims to form a government or call a fresh election. Such a possibility is said to have sent a shudder through Buckingham Palace, and urgent calls to constitutional experts.

On one topic the Queen has been remarkably outspoken: the Commonwealth, of which she is head. The famous Christmas broadcast of 1983, which saw HM (who is also Head of State of almost 20 lands outside the UK) chatting at length with Mrs Gandhi, brought right-wing protests. One satirist added that he had turned on half way through, and had thought he was watching a seasonal special by Hinge and Bracket.

Rumours persist of strained relations between Downing Street and the Palace. At a Balmoral picnic there were reports of a near-tussle over the teacups, when Mrs Thatcher could not accept that the Queen wanted to do the washing up. On another occasion a note was reportedly despatched from Downing Street, asking for details of the Royal outfit before each meeting, to avoid any embarrassment over clashing clothes. Back, it is said, came the reply: 'Her Majesty is not aware of what other people are wearing.'

Much was made of an alleged incident after the American-led invasion of Grenada (another of HM's territories). The Westminster grapevine insists that the Queen heard of the attack through a radio report, and summoned the Prime Minister – who sent back that she would be rather delayed.

The Queen replied that she was expected AT ONCE. Mrs Thatcher obeyed. Hurrying to their usual meeting room, she found that no chair had been provided for her use.

She had to explain her Government's inaction . . . while thinking on her feet.

St Margaret's The historic parish church of the Houses of Parliament, first honouring our dear Prime Minister several hundred years before her birth.

Sainsbury, Tim Ex-grocer Tim Sainsbury (Conservative, Hove) has deserted the super-rich family's anti-Tory faith – cousin David and father Lord Sainsbury still trust in Dr David Owen, after deserting Labour.

In a clan that has given much of its money away, boasts about personal wealth are regarded with suspicion and even scorn. But here, too, Tim Sainsbury parts company with his kin.

After the slashing of top-rate tax in Nigel Lawson's 1988 Budget, Mr Sainsbury couldn't resist gloating to colleagues about his huge windfall. 'There just aren't enough noughts on my pocket calculator to work out my winnings,' he confided.

Sang Froid During the depths of the Cold War, Harold Macmillan was addressing the Security Council of the United Nations. At one point amid the British politician's speech, Soviet leader Nikita Khrushchev disagreed so violently with the view being stated that he took off his shoe and banged it on the table in protest.

The dramatic scene sent a shock wave through the assembly, but not through Supermac. He languidly turned to an interpreter and asked: 'I wonder if I might have a translation?'

Scandal

> " The hurroosh that follows the intermittent revelation of the sexual goings-on of an unlucky MP has convinced me that the only safe pleasure for a Parliamentarian is a bag of boiled sweets. The alternative leads to the ultimate humiliation – to be pilloried on moral grounds by our popular Press. "

So wrote the Tory wit and MP Julian Critchley, but certain colleagues and political forebears – hooked on excitement and danger – have failed to agree with this. And even Mr Critchley remains open to attack. For encouraging dental decay.

Scramble The sight of MPs scrambling to their feet, holding in their stomachs and combing long wisps of hair over naked scalps can mean only one thing.

Miss World contestants have arrived on their annual trip to Westminster, and are waiting for guides to show them round.

SDP The Social Democratic Party founded by the Gang of Four became an SDP Gang of One, when Dr David Owen demurred on merger with the Liberals. The centrist grouping, still blessed with rich benefactors, also changed its nickname – from the Simply Divine Party (or even the Social Diseases Party) to the Sugar Daddies Party.

Secretaries Secretaries are the overworked and underpaid heroines of politics, who keep many Parliamentary careers afloat. When their employers are summarily ousted by the electorate, out they go too.

Pay and conditions for Commons secretaries have, admittedly, been somewhat improved of late. This is in large part due to a formidable association of secretarial staff at Westminster, which was formed to present a united front in the fight for fairer treatment. At one packed meeting there was massive support for a wide-ranging claim. A single voice was raised in opposition.

'If a secretary can't negotiate a good deal with her own MP then she doesn't deserve to be working at Westminster,' it said.

The speaker was Sara Keays, secretary to Tory Minister Cecil Parkinson.

Secrets

Although secrecy may be on the increase, it has always been popular in politics. MPs have liked to keep the details of their meetings to themselves since the days when they were terrified that the monarch might find out what they were saying and lock them up.

In 1771, the House of Commons summoned London newspaper printers who had dared to publish reports of debates and name Members who had spoken. The printers ignored the order. They were backed by the Corporation of the City of London, and the messenger whom the Serjeant at Arms had sent to arrest them was himself arrested when within the City's jurisdiction.

Then, in an original Whitehall farce, the Lord Mayor and an alderman – who also happened to be MPs – were admonished by the Speaker and committed to the Tower of London. There they soon became popular heroes. So Westminster never exerted its silencing authority again.

The House reluctantly accepted that its proceedings should be reported, but for many years journalists had to take their chance of crowding into the gallery with other visitors. Now they have their own Press Gallery, outside which the taking of notes and tape recordings is banned.

Even today, an MP has only to rise and say 'I spy strangers' and the House may resolve, after a division if necessary, that all non-Members be ordered to leave for the remainder of the session.

A further resolution is needed for a 'secret session', invoking statutory sanctions against the disclosure of proceedings. In peacetime this is a rarely used parliamentary ploy.

The Labour MP who 'spied strangers' in 1925, as a device to disconcert the Conservative Government, was dismayed to find that the Official Reporters had to leave as well. He ended up distraught that his brilliant verbal attacks had gone unrecorded.

The House of Lords set aside a special Press Gallery four years before the Commons; it was the first to use microphones and allow in radio recorders; and it has been televised since 1985. It seems curious that elected Members should have been the more anxious to hide their deliberations from the voters.

Sedgemore, Brian Leftist Brian Sedgemore (Labour, Hackney South and Shoreditch) is hard to miss in the House of Commons.

A barrister – who was asked to leave his chambers after passing legal documents to *Private Eye* – and an economist, he can launch brilliant assaults on capitalism and the Establishment.

On the other hand he is equally liable to bawl 'Arrogant bastards!' at his Tory opponents and leave it at that. For such behaviour he has been dubbed 'a boil on the bottom of the Labour Party' by Tory 1922 Committee chairman Cranley Onslow (Woking).

First elected for Luton in 1974, Mr Sedgemore was soon saying that a rumoured Heath-Thatcher reconciliation would be 'the love story of the century . . . the reunion of the harlot and the sailor.' He had meant 'monetarism' and 'Keynesianism' he later claimed. Either way, warning was served of many scathing attacks to come.

Serjeant at Arms The Serjeant at Arms is not a serjeant at all, but a retired senior officer drawn from each of the armed forces in turn. The present Serjeant is a major.

Clad in ceremonial garb with lace ruffles, silver buckles and knee breeches, the officer enforces order in the House of Commons and takes care of the Mace. His Upper House equivalent (*see* **Black Rod**) also looks as though he has just stepped out of a medieval pageant. He sports a thin-bladed sword and must hope that the mere sight of the weapon will persuade a wayward MP to quit the Chamber quietly. It will have been a long time since he last had any bayonet practice.

The Serjeant at Arms is in charge of a platoon of Doorkeepers who, with impressive silver-gilt badges of office round their necks, help him police the place. They must have completed 21 years in the forces, and reached the rank of Warrant Officer or Chief Petty Officer.

Anyone wanting to see his local MP can go to Westminster and fill in his name and address on a green card, which a Doorkeeper then takes round Westminster in search of the required Member. No doors are barred to this messenger until his quarry is captured. However, there are so many hiding places on the eight-acre site that an advance appointment is advisable.

The Serjeant at Arms tries to fit 650 MPs into a space designed for an anorexic 400. He is also responsible for keeping the Commons clean and clear of any modern-day Guy Fawkes, but delegates many duties to his staff.

When the Commons is sitting, he and three assistants must don fancy dress and take turns to sit in the Chamber at the Bar of the House. They are supposed to tear out tickets for two special boxes provided for friends of Privy Counsellors, but there are usually few takers.

So, providing MPs are settled and in peaceable mood, the Serjeant's main task during long hours of debate will lie in trying to stay awake.

'Seychellists' A conversation topic at Chelsea dinner parties, where Mr Kinnock and his Socialist supporters find little favour.

Skinner, Dennis Commons heckler Dennis Skinner (Labour), affectionately known as the Beast of Bolsover, has used as his targets virtually every other MP in the House of Commons. Almost all, including Tony Benn on occasion, have been judged not left-wing enough. After several attacks Dennis the Menace has been given his marching orders from the Chamber (as when he accused David Owen of being a 'sod', or claimed that the Prime Minister might try to bribe judges in the GCHQ union case).

The usual Skinner style of speech is a bellow. He may have had useful training in voice projection during his mining days, when he also worked as a club singer – with imitations of Al Johnson his speciality.

SLD

The Social and Liberal Democrats were born from a desire to merge the middle in British politics and avoid the unfortunate initials LSD. Although they hope to be dubbed Democrats, SLD supporters have so far been saddled with acronyms. The 'soiled' or 'sold-out' party have proved more popular than their preferred 'solid' party tag.

One Westminster wit has also labelled the party 'Parliamentarians' salads', because 'some of them are green, most of them are poorly dressed and all of them are soggy'.

Clement Freud once suggested that the grouping might be called the Social Democratic/Liberal Alliance Party, which could be shortened to the Sod-em-all Party, but this helpful idea found few backers.

Slogans

As television now largely dictates the conduct of election campaigns, instant images are musts for parties vying for power. And catchy slogans are more crucial than ever. Huge sums are paid to advertising companies to dream up a memorable message, in six words or less.

The Liberal Party was certainly in need of outside help in 1974, when it came close to fighting under the electoral banner 'One More Heave'. Also considered was 'We're All In It Together'. Perhaps both could have been adopted, along with a third – 'Throw Up A Liberal Government'.

Not for a long time have the election-losing Liberals been held to their slogan promises. But party legend recalls the 1885 General Election, when they fought under the banner 'Three acres and a cow'. One voter in rural Somerset arrived with a halter at his polling station and said: 'I voted Liberal. I'll take the cow back with me now.'

Smears

What the other parties say and do.

Smith, Sir Cyril

Still a formidable force on his rare trips to Westminster, Cyril Smith (SLD, Rochdale) has scant regard for the Commons. 'I treat it with great disdain,' he says.

Rochdale's most famous export since Gracie Fields, and far bulkier, Big Cyril has also put his view more bluntly. Within days of his first election victory he had branded Parliament 'the end of the pier . . . a daft political charade.'

He later revised his opinion, declaring, 'This place is the longest-running farce in the West End.'

Snap Decisions

Some MPs take a lot of time to make up their minds, others do it in a trice.

Among the quick-thinkers is Geoffrey Dickens (Conservative, Littleborough and Saddleworth), a nineteen-stone former boxer. At a Press conference to allege a cover-up in a child porn case, the outspoken Member also announced to astonished journalists that he was leaving his family for a divorcée in Tunbridge Wells.

One reporter asked the MP when he had decided to walk out on his wife, two teenage sons and a paddock of show-jumpers named after characters in Charles Dickens novels.

'I am sorry to say, only this moment,' came the reply. He intended to go straight from the meeting to telephone the affected parties!

Gentle readers will be relieved to hear that the vocal upholder of moral values has now returned to the family fold.

Snuff

Should you hear an outbreak of sneezing and spluttering in the Commons Chamber, or espy a mass fluttering of silk handker-

chiefs, do not be alarmed. It is almost certainly not early warning of a flu epidemic. Rather, Honourable Members will have been helping themselves to a Parliamentary perk . . .

Smoking is banned in the Chamber. So, just outside the entrance, in a wooden box next to the head doorkeeper, is a supply of snuff. It's a thoughtful alternative for passing MPs who need a quick fix.

Soames, Nicholas Nicholas 'Bunter' Soames (Conservative, Crawley) is the latest of the Churchill line to pursue a career in politics. So far, however, the great man's grandson has been more noted for the colour of his clothes than his speeches. Indeed, Mr Soames was once accused of disrupting Parliamentary business while sitting silently on the green benches of the Commons Chamber. The loudness of his suit was said to be to blame.

A typical Soames wheeze was when he turned up for work wearing a tie stamped with the image of Superman, complete with cloak, tights and underpants worn on the outside. The face, however, was unmistakably that of the Honourable Member for Crawley. And to press the point home the tie was emblazoned with the legend 'Supernick'.

Accused of childish habits by his political enemies, Mr Soames also fell foul of a Select Committee rule that members may not read newspapers during proceedings. Castigated with another colleague for appearing to do just that, the young Tory protested that his reading matter was relevant to the topic under discussion.

Brian Wilson (Labour, Cunninghame North) came to his aid. At least Mr Soames wasn't trying to colour his in, he told the chairman.

Songsters It is rare for politicians to burst into song. Unless they are of Celtic stock. Neil Kinnock and other Welsh MPs are on occasions keen to display the strength of their close-harmony singing.

And the Scots have the impishly musical Scottish National Party. Tartan Tory Nicholas Fairbairn once wagged a finger at the three SNP MPs and boomed 'And just remember this. . .'.

'A kiss is just a kiss,' the trio then mockingly chorused.

The Speaker The most powerful person in the House of Commons is not the Prime Minister – who need not even be a Member of that House – but the Speaker, who chairs sessions after being elected by MPs (*see* **Swearing In**).

An effective Speaker combines honesty, firmness, fairness, good humour and an ability to abandon party ties. Few MPs are so blessed.

The Speaker currently enjoys a salary of £52,798 and a magnificent residence in the Palace of Westminster; he can also look forward to a generous pension and usually a peerage. As there is no such thing as a free flat in politics, the Speaker has to work colossal hours – chairing Parliamentary sittings which may run late into the night, conferring with staff, dealing with correspondence and meeting MPs.

He must be able to identify the 649 Members who will seek to catch his eye to speak; a recall of their main interests is required, too. And he must further familiarise himself with the topics to be raised at Question Time and in debate each day.

The Speaker is expected to maintain an orderly House – keeping debaters to the point and being prepared to order seriously wayward MPs to leave the Chamber (*see* **Naming**).

Retaining his constituency links, the Speaker faces re-election with his colleagues and is invariably returned. There is periodic pressure for a special phantom constituency for him, but electors do not appear unduly worried by the loss of a party label. They seem to know that any government will ensure that constituency grievances raised by the Speaker receive the speediest attention.

So far the office has been a male preserve. But this barrier could soon be broken. One of our three Deputy Speakers at present is Betty Boothroyd (Labour, West Bromwich West), whose high-stepping kick might offer a novel means of keeping order in the Chamber. Miss Boothroyd was formerly a Tiller Girl.

Speaker's Chop During the 19th century, and for a brief period in the 1920s, a Speaker's Chop was an unofficial adjournment of the House which allowed the hard-pressed Speaker to have his dinner. Nowadays, the Speaker can be relieved by a deputy at any time, so debates continue while he snatches a meal.

According to Sir Henry Lucy, a Member who was mentally deranged once went behind the Chair and 'tried to eat the Speaker's chop!' He must have returned a disappointed man.

Speaker's Procession Visitors are awed daily by the sight of the Speaker's Procession wending its way from the officer's private quarters – via the Lower Waiting Hall, Central Lobby and Members' Lobby – to the Chamber a few minutes before the sitting is due to begin with prayers.

It consists of the Bar Doorkeeper (who sets the pace), the Serjeant at Arms carrying the Mace, the Speaker, his Train-bearer, his Secretary and his Chaplain. All being in court or formal dress, they make an impressive picture.

In case spectators aren't feeling sufficiently respectful as the party passes through Central Lobby, a senior police officer shouts 'Hats off, Strangers!' That normally does the trick.

The occasion has a military feel and a former Speaker, W. S. Morrison, once admitted that he hummed under his breath a favourite march of regimental pipes and drums, 'The Barren Rocks of Aden'. He had worked out, with military precision, that the tune lasted the exact distance from his private quarters to the Chair.

Speech One part content, nine parts delivery.

A Conservative candidate who once said 'The Tory Government will do nothing without consulting the parents' paused after 'nothing' and reduced his audience to hysterics.

Similarly Roy (now Lord) Jenkins' confession that he left the Labour Party without 'wegwet or wancour' was not thought wise.

In Parliament, politicians may refer to notes. But if they are obviously reciting from a prepared text, unless they happen to be Ministers, their wise words are likely to be interrupted by contemptuous cries of 'Reading!' This tends to reduce the impact of their delivery.

Lord Mancroft once observed, 'A speech is like a love affair: any fool can start one but to end it requires considerable skill.' There is, in fact, no absolute rule about length of contributions in the Commons Chamber except in major debates – where backbenchers are restricted to a ten minute maximum. Pressure of time means that a humble backbencher is lucky to last 20 minutes (while Ministers may make an hour).

The House will forgive almost anything except insults, irrelevance and tedious repetition. Providing he remains technically 'in order', a bore will be allowed to continue until even he is stupified into silence.

However, a debate can be stopped in full flow if an MP rises and moves 'that the question be now put'. Should the Speaker agree, at least 100 Members must back such a 'closure' move, if it is to be imposed on a resistant minority. This device was first used in 1881, by Speaker Brand, when Irish MPs were still rising to speak after the House had sat for a record 41 hours.

As Clement Attlee put it: 'Democracy means government by discussion. But it is only effective if you can stop people talking.' For the ultimate sanction against garrulous MPs, *see* **Guillotine**.

Stamina Today's statesmen and women seem to share Harold Wilson's view that a week is a long time in politics. Stamina and staying power look to be declining fast.

The present Father of the House, Sir Bernard Braine, was a mere 72 when he succeeded to the title of our longest-serving male MP, in 1987. It is unlikely that Sir Bernard will better the record Charles Pelham Villiers, Conservative Member for Wolverhampton South when he died, aged 96, in January 1898. He had been an MP for 63 years, having been returned at 17 elections.

The longest recorded Parliamentary span in British history was that of Sir Francis Knollys (c1550–1648). He was elected MP for Oxford in 1575 and died as the sitting Member for Reading, 73 years later, in 1648.

Statesman 'A statesman is an ex-politician who has mastered the art of holding his tongue.' (Anon.)

Steel, David A cottager in the Scottish borders was once astonished to open his door, at dead of night, to find local MP David Steel in full jester's costume. The then Liberal leader and his wife, who

was clad as a medieval wench, had broken down in their car while returning from a fancy dress ball.

The politician's troubles with transport continued when he got out of a train on the wrong side, and almost plunged to the track. On another occasion, convinced that a train stop gave him time to leap out and buy a snack, he was left stranded on a Midland platform, hamburger in hand.

Such stories confirm the human, even fallible image of David Steel on which so much of his popularity has rested – at least before he was savaged by the makers of *Spitting Image*.

Though a steely tactician, the architect of the Social and Liberal Democrats has been hampered by a certain shyness (say his friends) or aloofness (say his enemies) in public. For the antis, Cyril Smith has charged: 'He couldn't make a bang if he had a firework in each hand.'

Stokes, John

John Stokes (Conservative, Halesowen and Stourbridge) is a rare survivor, along with Julian Amery (Conservative, Brighton Pavilion), of a once-great strain of Tory. One commentator summed him up as a '100 per cent wholemeal reactionary, for whom the 20th century has been a mistake.' His plan for solving a certain industrial dispute was to 'shoot a few ringleaders'.

Mr Stokes once moaned that old-fashioned restraint had been replaced by the 'sinister suggestion that everyone is having sexual intercourse with everyone else all the time'. He also sniffed that the Gas Board's 'share a bath' campaign during the 1974 fuel crisis was 'vulgar'.

Swearing In

The election of a Speaker – Chairman in the Commons Chamber – is the first act of a new Parliament. So from the start the scene is set for the medieval melodrama which colours so much of the work of Westminster.

At 2.30 pm sharp – everything in Parliament begins promptly at 2.30 pm, though endings are far less certain – the Father of the House takes the Chair. Black Rod, the peers' equivalent of the Serjeant at Arms, then advances from the House of Lords to find a typically warm British greeting awaiting him at the House of Commons. The door is slammed in his face and he must knock three times before it is opened again. This is to remind him that the Commons does not like being bossed about by the Lords.

That said, or rather unsaid, the Father of the House and a large posse of MPs traipse dutifully off to the Lords, where three gentlemen in black tricorn hats command them to elect a

Speaker. They meekly obey, turning tail and returning to the Commons.

After speeches by the 'Mover' and 'Seconder' as to why their nominee should be accepted, the Commons usually agrees. This is because the parties will have decided beforehand who is the best bet for the job. If a Speaker does not have the confidence of both sides, the Chamber will soon sink into noisy disorder and the Chair will soon be hoarse.

Once chosen, Mr Speaker Elect acts as though the whole thing has come as a huge shock to him – and perhaps it has. He must be dragged into the Chair from where, bowing to the inevitable, he reluctantly makes a little 'thank you' speech.

Tired after so much excitement, the House adjourns with the Principal Doorkeeper shouting 'Who goes home?' and answering himself with 'Usual time tomorrow'. It is unclear why he does this but, coming from an ex-military man, the instruction is barked with force and conviction.

The next day the House meets with the Speaker clad in bob wig, court dress but no gown. He sits in the Chair and Black Rod arrives, only to be locked out again – in case the message delivered 24 hours earlier still hasn't got through.

The Commons then marches to the Lords, where the Lord Chancellor, on behalf of the Queen, approves the Speaker. There would be a collective gasp and a constitutional crisis if he didn't. Then everyone marches back again. The Speaker goes to the Chair and puts on his gown. (The current holder of the post, Speaker Weatherill, is a former tailor and so quite used to the idea of dressing in public.)

The poor Serjeant at Arms, who has been carting the Mace around all this time, thankfully places the heavy object on the Table and retires. Oaths or (non-religious) affirmations of allegiance are then taken. The penalties for ducking out are laid down in the Parliamentary Oath Act of 1966: 'If after the Speaker has been chosen a Member votes or sits during any debate without having taken the oath or made the affirmation he is liable to a fine not exceeding £500 for each offence, and his seat is vacated as if he were dead!'

Having gone to such pains to reach the Commons, even the most rebellious and revolutionary MP is prepared to queue for however long is needed.

An MP of religious bent recites the words 'I swear by Almighty God that I will be faithful and bear true allegiance to Her Majesty Queen Elizabeth, her heirs and successors according to Law, so help me God.' An atheist may state that he solemnly, sincerely and truly declares and affirms his allegiance to Her Majesty the Queen. While God is dispensable in this instance, the monarch is not. Republicans have to bite the bullet, or face bankruptcy and the loss of their jobs.

Taxes Payments switching wealth from the rich to the poor – and sometimes vice versa – and which keep politicians in business.

Setting levels of levy to ensure enough revenue and quell complaints is a taxing task. As was recognised long ago by Jean Baptiste Colbert (1619–83), who said, 'The art of taxation consists in so plucking a goose as to obtain the largest possible amount of feathers, with the smallest possible amount of hissing.'

The US writer Mark Twain (1835–1910) made a bitter joke of the subject. 'What is the difference between a taxidermist and a tax collector?' he asked, before answering himself: 'The taxidermist takes only your skin.'

Nothing changes. But then, as the philosopher Edmund Burke wrote in 1774, 'To tax and to please, no more than to love and be wise, is not given to men.'

Tea Room Divided along party lines, this House of Commons institution finds Labour MPs seated nearest the door. The Tea Room is a place of plots, gossip and buttered crumpets. Ministers, including the Premier, are often to be found here mingling with the workers and gauging the mood of the party.

Not always liking what they hear, they sometimes leave with chronic indigestion.

The Tea Room saw one of the celebrated exchanges of the last election campaign, when Labour shadow spokesman John Prescott bitterly accused former leader Jim (now Lord) Callaghan of nuking the party's prospects by savaging its stance on defence. Commander-in-chief Neil Kinnock dismissed the tiff as a storm in a tea room, but gales of gleeful laughter swept through Conservative Central Office.

Tebbit, Norman Gaunt spokesman of the working-class Tory, Norman Tebbit (Conservative, Chingford) delights in snide and savage speeches. Venomous invective has earned the veteran hardliner such labels as the 'Chingford Strangler' (Julian Critchley), a 'semi house-trained polecat' (Michael Foot) or 'the Prime Minister's pet piranha' (John Grant).

But the former ultra-loyal Minister, who fell out with Mrs Thatcher over his handling of the last Conservative election campaign, is now a rightist rebel who roams about collecting city directorships and political scalps at will.

There is, however, a gentle side to Mr Tebbit and a refreshing line in self-parody, though chiefly in private.

When Trade and Industry Secretary, he once gave an interview to journalists in his office, flanked by senior civil servant advisers. One reporter asked the workaholic: 'What do you do in your spare time?' Before Norman Tebbit could reply, an aide chipped in: 'He bites the heads off chickens.' The Minister guffawed with laughter.

Ted Ted the dogged old campaigner is dead. Heavy-jowled, he was until recently a figure of fun in the Commons Chamber, where he could be found snoring gently during most debates. When awake, he couldn't resist growling his contempt for the present occupants of the Conservative front bench – once even letting out a bark of protest when Norman Tebbit stood up to speak.

In his energetic prime Ted enjoyed attending concerts, sailing on the Solent and trotting through the high offices of public life. In his later years, scandalously denied his rightful place in the House of Lords, he dozed and dreamed.

Ted was, of course, the guide dog of David Blunkett MP (Sheffield Brightside), Labour's blind visionary.

Ten Minute Rule Bill A backbench MP stands little chance of getting a pet project on to the Statute Book. Government and Opposition have a monopoly over Parliamentary time, which largely ensures that individual Members do not get in their way.

Twice a week, however, time is still allowed for an MP to bring in a Ten Minute Rule Bill. This gives the Member moving a motion, and others in reply, the chance to make their views known. Provided they can do it within ten minutes.

The glory generally ends there. For however good their argument, the proposal still has to take its turn behind all other Private Members' Bills which have been debated before. Such Bills are chosen by ballot for Friday morning debate. Only the highest two or three are likely to succeed because of the limited number of Friday mornings in each session, and the pressure for space in committee rooms where consideration of the measures must continue.

The humble backbencher's only other hope is that the Government might decide to support the mooted measure, and agree to take the topic on board in its pending legislative programme. It pays to be on good terms with the party in power.

Thatcher, Denis Businessman Denis Thatcher inherited a lot of money and made a great deal more. He also married famously. Though happiest when watching golf, rugby and ice dissolving in a large gin and tonic, the stalwart gent provides his spouse with stoic support.

Mr Thatcher is said to be rather more politically robust than his wife, but refuses to be drawn on his exact views. To one inquiry he replied that he never made public announcements on anything. 'That way I don't get into trouble.'

Thatcher, Margaret (I) Divorced ex-wife of Denis Thatcher. Now living in quiet anonymity.

Thatcher, Margaret (II) Mrs Thatcher, the one who has been Britain's longest-serving Prime Minister this century, modestly informed her biographer that she had 'changed everything'.

The Premier was certainly right as far as the healing words of St Francis of Assisi are concerned, which she misquoted on the steps of 10 Downing Steet after her first election win in 1979.

Ever plain-spoken, Lord (Jim) Prior says: 'From her lips they (the saint's words) were the most awful humbug.'

Thatcher-speak

As one who has dominated the political scene like few before her, Margaret Thatcher weighs every word carefully. Her famous skill at cutting away the flab from a given argument, and her fighting talk at moments of stress, have produced a string of verbal pearls. Such as:

'Just rejoice! Rejoice!'
Mrs Thatcher's suggestion on how Britons should react to news of the retaking of South Georgia during the Falklands conflict. The celebrants did not include the Archbishop of Canterbury at a subsequent war memorial service in St Paul's Cathedral.

'Frit!'
A Lincolnshire word for 'lack of bottle', which a female native of the county has been known to repeat at volume when standing at the Commons Despatch Box and berating the Labour benches.

'We'
First person singular for the House of Windsor. The current occupant of 10 Downing Street has also been known to use the word, but whether it was meant to embrace the entire Government, the Conservative Party, Herself and Mr Denis Thatcher – or signify delusions of Royal grandeur – remains a moot point.

'I was on holiday at the time'
Mrs Thatcher's famous assertion, backing her claim of being uninformed during the Westland saga, that modern telecommunications had yet to penetrate the Alps.

'I want my money back!'
Slamming her handbag on to a summit table, Mrs Thatcher explains the intricacies of her policies on the European Community.

'I've never understood men'
The Prime Minister encounters opposition at a European summit.

'Only the French could do that'
Britain's present Premier emerges from a Euro-battle in Brussels – which, after all, is very close to Waterloo. She may still be smarting from the Paris opinion poll which named her France's most unpopular foreign leader, ahead of Libyan Colonel Gadaffi and Ayatollah Khomeini of Iran.

Thorpe, Jeremy

One of the last acts of the self-destructing (or merging) Liberal Party occurred when party leaders met at the National Liberal Club to dedicate a room to the memory of one of their greatest forebears, David Lloyd George.

They also unveiled a portrait to a less illustrious former leader who was known for vaulting fences and getting stuck in hovercrafts, and who got into all sorts of trouble when hounded by a former male model named Norman Scott.

Yes, Jeremy Thorpe was being rehabilitated at the historic heart of Liberalism, with a belated portrait in his honour. But the opening didn't quite run as smoothly as had been planned.

A senior officer of the club recalled in an unfortunate speech that he had once overheard one Liberal asking another what should be done with Jeremy Thorpe. 'I'd like to hang him,' came the reply.

And that, added the official, in Mr Thorpe's presence, was what they were going to do.

Titles

In order to promote the cause of civilised Commons debate, and to cut down on the risk of giving offence, sparking uproar and even spilling blood, an MP is not allowed to refer to another as 'You' or to mention an Honourable Member by name. Breach of this rule will provoke speedy intervention from the Speaker.

Such a regulation in no way rescues MPs who cannot put names to the faces of their colleagues. For they must instead refer to constituencies, which can be even more difficult to remember – thanks to the regular, name-changing machinations of the Boundary Commission.

If a Parliamentary opponent is being spoken of, he will be referred to as 'The Honourable Member for Great Snoring'. Or if a colleague from the same side, he will be 'My Honourable Friend, the Member for Great Snoring'. Unless, of course, he is an Honourable Lady.

If the MP being mentioned is a Privy Counsellor he becomes 'My Right Honourable Friend' (or 'The Right Honourable Member'). If he is a barrister of the Queen's Counsel variety, he is deemed to be an 'Honourable and Learned Member'. Quite why such an MP should be assumed learned, constitutional experts are at a loss to explain.

If an MP has been a professional soldier he is an 'Honourable and Gallant Member' even if a veteran of the catering corps. And if he boasts a courtesy title, he will be 'My Honourable and Noble Friend'.

Hardest of all references is to an MP of wide experience, who happens to be a Privy Counsellor, a Queen's Counsel and a soldier. 'My Right Honourable, Learned and Gallant Friend, the Member for Great Snoring,' doesn't exactly roll off the tongue.

MPs have just about fathomed out how to refer to their 649 colleagues when it's time for another election, heralding another huge intake of unknown faces.

Tories A term that used to apply to parties of Irish bandits. But, over the centuries, it has come to have a political connection as well.

U-turns Ever since Mrs Thatcher declared that 'The lady's not for turning', Opposition politicians have pleaded even harder for policy U-turns.

Occasionally, when faced with a big backbench revolt and uproar in the country, the Iron Lady has bent. Only to draw howls of derision from the Labour benches.

Such scenes have stiffened the Premier's resolve never to do it again.

Venison Senior whips and Cabinet Ministers are rewarded each year with a haunch of venison from the Royal Park at Richmond – as a gracious reminder, perhaps, that the Palace of Westminster is held only on lease from the Crown.

In order to earn his haunch one of the senior whips, who glories in the ancient title of Vice-chamberlain of the Household, has to précis for the Queen the daily doings of the Commons. The poor chap may find that this task takes up most of his afternoon.

As yet there is no provision for a vegetarian alternative to this carnivorous perk, but Prince Charles may wish for innovation here.

Victory Sign Two fingers raised aloft, palm outward, can mark a triumph of Churchillian scale. Or, reversed, the sign can mean something altogether ruder. Both versions have been tried by excited politicians.

V Vote Early, Vote Often

Environment Secretary Nicholas Ridley was accused of making the latter gesture to Tory MPs, who had just staged an unsuccessful backbench revolt against his poll tax plans. One ally suggested that the Minister had in fact been waving to friends in the gallery – though what they could have done to upset him is anyone's guess.

As leader of the Opposition, Mrs Thatcher was visiting Rome when news came through of a famous by-election victory. She instinctively gave what was intended as the two-fingered Churchillian greeting, but got the gesture the wrong way round. Newspapers the next day carried pictures of the Tory chief appearing to flash a surprising message to the President of Italy, who stood at her side.

Vote Early, Vote Often The slogan behind 99 per cent turnouts in Northern Ireland, where the dead miraculously rise up and walk to the polling station. Some even make it twice.

One former Northern Ireland Minister tells the tale of accompanying a distinguished MP on a trip to a hard-pressed part of his constituency. As they alighted from the ministerial limo a crowd of angry women advanced. The MP was all set to meet them, until one shouted, 'I voted for you 18 times at the last election, and what have you done for me?'

At that he scarpered, sharpish.

Walker, Peter The appointment of the wettest of the Wets (Conservative, Worcester) as Secretary of State for Wales did not signify glaring ignorance of geography by the Conservative leadership in London.

After the last election rout of Tories in the Principality, Mr Walker was the nearest survivor of any stature.

Peter Walker plainly agreed that the Welsh Marches were as near to Wales as made no difference. For he promptly picked as his Parliamentary Private Secretary Colin Shepherd, Tory MP for Hereford.

At the Welsh Office, the man who once boasted that he would be super-rich by his 30th birthday – and who managed to earn £500,000 with months to spare – has set up a sort of Heathite Cabinet in exile. His department alone secured a substantial increase in its cash allocation for 1988–89, receiving every penny the Minister asked for.

Mrs Thatcher is more noted for putting Tory Wets through the wringer. Why should Peter Walker be spared? Could it have anything to do with the moderate's convincing Ted Heath to keep at least one woman in his pre-1970 Shadow Cabinet? Mr Walker had also recommended that the space be filled by a certain Margaret Thatcher.

Mr Heath has been able to regret his acceptance at leisure, but for Mr Walker the decision may have proved a lifeline.

WASPS Men of the WASPish (White Anglo Saxon Protestant) variety once dominated the House of Commons. But during the Thatcher decade most have been turned into drones.

Wastepaper Over two and a half tons of wastepaper are collected each week from the Palace of Westminster, most having originated as documents and order papers from the Vote Office of the Commons or the Printed Paper Office in the Lords.

Europe now provides a rival source of mega-reams of waste-paper. When Britain joined the Common Market in 1973, every MP was entitled to 42 volumes detailing EEC regulations to date. Few felt moved to claim such compulsive bedtime reading. Which was just as well, as each set cost the taxpayer £143.

Ways and Means Deputy Speaker Harold Walker (Labour, Doncaster Central) delights in the ancient title of Chairman of Ways and Means. The post – entitling the holder to preside over the Commons when it considers finance bills, for instance – once carried greater weight than it does now.

Indeed, it has become much misunderstood. The Deputy Speaker recently received an invoice from his vintner, addressed to 'Mr H Walker, chairman of Wear and Mens'.

This may have been a case of mistaken identity. For although Harold Walker is the son of a hatmaker, Speaker Weatherill is a qualified master tailor.

Weight The trend towards healthy eating has taken off among certain politicians, who worry about spreading waistlines more than most. As there is a glaring lack of physical exercise in the average political day, such concern is often felt with good reason.

But at times weight has been a distinct advantage. In one 17th-century division, for instance, teller Lord Grey jokingly counted an outsize peer as being worth ten votes rather than one.

When his companion teller, Lord Norris, failed to spot the jest, Lord Grey decided to let the ten votes stand. With the result that a Bill which the House had actually rejected was put down as being passed.

Wets Tory critics of the Thatcherite creed, who all but evaporated when the heat was turned on.

Whipping Not (or at least seldom) the sort that has made Streatham famous. True, MPs can sometimes be seen heading furtively towards a Commons outbuilding, where a room has been kitted out with instruments of torture of every kind. But this gruesome chamber is known as The Gym.

Party managers (licensed by the leader) like to maintain discipline over their MPs by rather more subtle means than direct physical punishment although, on odd occasions, angry scenes have ended in blows.

When a new MP arrives at Westminster, the Chief Whip indicates in no uncertain terms that any intention of voting against the party line must be signalled well in advance. Or the eager entrant can whistle for promotion. Being men and women of not a little ambition, thrusting MPs normally heed these warning words.

There is more than the lash in the whips' armoury. Besides recommending Parliamentary Private Secretaries – the lowest rung on the governmental ladder – and Junior Ministers to the Premier, they also nominate for knighthoods and for many other recognitions of service to the monarch beloved by most Britons. Patronage proves a powerful weapon. Whips compile the list of those invited to join the most coveted foreign delegations – to study the Seychelles tourist industry, for instance, or a trade mission to Brazil that just happens to coincide with carnival time.

And these party policemen can even deny a wayward MP the use of a desk or telephone in the overcrowded House of Commons. So it pays not to upset them. Especially as, like elephants, they never forget.

Aided by an anonymous but senior civil servant, known to all as the 'Usual Channels', whips aim to ensure the smooth passage of government business. Though their opposition counterparts seek to frustrate this wish – keeping a bottle of champagne in a padlocked fridge in case of special victories – it is not in their long-term interests to violate courtly Commons procedure. And many deals are fixed between supposedly diehard opponents in the area located (and dubbed) 'Behind the Speaker's Chair'.

While a good whip appears charming and cheerful to all, he must also be capable of cold-blooded ruthlessness. Before the closest and most crucial votes, the sick will receive a callous summons. More than one MP has been stretchered into the Commons to save a government's skin. Mercifully, provided a Member is within the precincts of the Palace of Westminster, he can be counted. The fate of a 19th-century government, led by Lord Melbourne, once depended on the House doctor's judgment as to whether an MP was still breathing at the time of the vote. The medic's verdict kept Lord Melbourne's administration alive.

Whitelaw, Viscount (Willie)

A former deputy Prime Minister and Cabinet stalwart, Lord Whitelaw is still loved by all for his kind nature and verbal gems. Getting as close as he ever could to anger, the Tory politician once accused Labour leaders of 'going about the country stirring up apathy'.

Even when the noble peer turned a pheasant shoot into a peasant shoot, and mistakenly peppered a brace of beaters with stray pellets, the injured parties insisted that they couldn't have been maimed by a finer gent.

Williams, Shirley

The woman whose hair and appearance tend to suggest that she has just suffered a severe electric shock – the sort of look, according to writer Dame Rebecca West, that could only have been instilled at a 'really good' girls' school.

Although rivalling Margaret Thatcher as the most popular female politician of our times, such support did not stop her from losing at the 1979, 1983 and 1987 General Elections. In three different seats.

In the rather sour memoirs of her brother, John Catlin, she was said to have been mortified as a teenager by the splendour of the family's home in Cheyne Walk, Chelsea. The young Shirley would use the tradesmen's entrance, as though she were the daughter of the housekeeper and it might be 'the door into the Labour Party', her sibling seethed.

Unlike Mrs T, the Socialist-turned-Democrat Mrs Williams makes frequent use of public transport. And, despite her legendary lateness, she claims never to have missed a train in her life.

W Witchcraft

Witchcraft There are frequent charges that the darker corners of politics are rife with the lodges of freemasonry, but rumours of witches' covens are rare. They might have been non-existent, had it not been for Geoffrey Dickens (Conservative, Littleborough and Saddleworth), the obese campaigner for maverick causes.

Here is a relevant extract from *Hansard* recording the MP's accusation of sorcery in a spellbound House of Commons:

> **Mr Geoffrey Dickens:** Will the Leader of the House set aside time for a debate on the workings of the Fraudulent Mediums Act 1951, which replaced the Witchcraft Act 1735?. . . We need a chance to discuss the working of witchcraft and how it can be controlled in this country. (Laughter.) People laughed when I spoke nine years ago about child abuse. Those people are now listening, and I am warning the House that witchcraft is sweeping the country.
>
> **Mr Dennis Skinner (Bolsover):** It is in Downing Street.
>
> **Mr Speaker:** Order. This is a serious question.

Indeed it is. Supporters of Mr Skinner believe that demonic doings in Downing Street may explain why so many Tory MPs have been turned into toadies.

Wives Still an essential tool of the trade for most successful Tory politicians. They are expected to act as nurse, psychiatrist, hostess, secretary, constituency organiser and stand-in at fundraising functions when hubbie has been called away to a vital engagement at his golf club.

The unwritten *Good Wife Guide*, passed by word of mouth to any serious aspirant to the job, adds that an ability to gaze adoringly at the spouse during his endless renditions of the same speech is also vital.

Other parties are far less demanding on their wives, or 'house partners' as *The Guardian* readers among them may prefer. An appearance at the annual constituency beanfeast should be enough.

Of course, a Good Wife can help enormously in the transformation from politician to statesman. While from Downing Street Mary Wilson wrote poetry wistful for privacy, and Audrey Callaghan continued to dress as if for gardening, birds of paradise such as Clemmie Churchill took to the demands of public displays – well, like ducks to water.

Proudest and most brilliant of them all was Margot Asquith, whose glamour and gorgeous wit shocked not a few in her otherwise prudish times. She adored gossip, once describing a distinguished lady as 'a dear friend, but rather careless with her body'.

Margot never pulled her punchlines in public. She frankly admitted, for example, that she and the Prime Minister had sleeping problems: 'I like heat without weight. Henry likes weight without heat. I sleep under a couple of Shetland shawls. Henry would be happy stark naked under a grand piano.'

In these days of She Who Must Be Obeyed, a growing number of politicians' husbands are learning how to set their smiles. (*See* **Thatcher, Denis**)

But few indeed are the couples whose partners are equally set on high political office. Most homes would be too small to hold two outsize egos. As Nancy Astor and Winston Churchill acknowledged in their now famous exchange:

'Winston, if I were married to you I'd put poison in your coffee.'

'Nancy, if you were my wife, I'd drink it.'

Women This half of the species was long a rare sight at Westminster, even after votes for women were conceded from 1918.

An initial ban on ladies in the Commons Chamber was gradually relaxed until 1778, when an Honourable Gentleman complained during a debate that women were seated while some of his male friends were forced to stand. The early feminists resisted a resulting order for their removal. Some put up a brave struggle for all of two hours.

After that, the ban was back with a vengeance. So much so that Mrs Sheridan had to don male attire to get in to hear her husband's speeches. Until, 50 years later, ladies were admitted to a room above the Chamber, where they were allowed to peer through an iron grating above the House chandelier.

Following the 1834 fire, and amid much opposition, a gallery was constructed for up to 24 women. It was partitioned off and screened in front by open trellis work lest any disturbance be created. Even this cage was closed for 20 years when, in 1888, certain ladies had the cheek to applaud a speech. But when women won the vote, the trellis work symbolically came down, and other political barriers slowly fell.

Not that the first elected female MP was able to claim her seat. Sinn Fein's Countess Markievicz was being detained at His Majesty's pleasure at the time and was thus disqualified. Even when released from Holloway she refused a transfer to Westminster as a Republican protest.

So Tory by-election victor Nancy Astor became the first woman Member to make it into the House of Commons. Margaret Thatcher, heading a record 41 female victors at the last election, recently unveiled a plaque in her honour.

Though their styles differ – it would be hard to imagine Mrs Thatcher performing cartwheels to cheer up the bombed-out citizens of Plymouth – the Prime Minister saluted a kindred spirit who had shown determination, courage and 'a proper sense of her own views'.

The Premier also revealed that she returns shortlists of candidates for top jobs to her officials if they contain no woman's name. But clearly, this rule is relaxed when it comes to selecting her Cabinet.

ZZZZZZZZZ Z

The Woolsack The Woolsack was recently restuffed with fresh shearings after Lord Hailsham went down with a nasty dose of Lord Chancellor's Bottom. Such a numbing condition affects those who have sat on the square, lumpy couch for far too long.

For some odd reason the Woolsack, which stands in front of the Throne in the Lords' Chamber, is regarded as being 'outside the House'. When the Lord Chancellor wishes to make a speech he must rise and move a couple of paces to his left. Although this places him on the Opposition side of the House, his address is that of a key member of the Cabinet. Tradition need not be logical.

X X is how you vote.

The method arose at a time when most people could make no other mark on paper and, although the majority of us can now manage most of the letters of the alphabet, we are still stuck with it. This is because such a simple first-past-the-post system allows a single party winning a minority of votes to form a government outright.

Listing candidates in numbered preferences, like much of Europe, seems as alien as changing miles to kilometres. Smaller groups, however, have good cause to cry 'murder'.

Youngest Member The youngest member of the present House of Lords should have been Prince Charles. HRH was technically eligible to take his seat at the age of three, when he became Duke of Cornwall – but wisely he waited before bowling his maiden speech, on sport and leisure. Until he was 25, in fact.

The youngest recorded MP was one Henry Long (1420–90), who was returned for an Old Sarum seat at the sage age of fifteen. Minors were barred from the House of Commons in 1832, when the rottenest borough of Old Sarum was also abolished.

'You've Never Had It So Good' From the outcry that followed his famous retort to a heckler, Prime Minister Harold Macmillan learnt the hard way that the British are essentially a nostalgic race. Yearning for days of yore need not entail accurate memories. After all, how many of today's admirers of Victorian Values are fondly recalling workhouses, jingoism and typhoid?

ZZZZZZZZZ If in the Commons Chamber you spot an MP sprawled across a bench, he is most likely listening to a microphone cunningly concealed low down in the seat-back. Others, with eyes closed, may be meditating on a pressing political problem. But inevitably, the odd Member may have decided to sleep on it.